MANAGING TIME

A How-To-Do-It Manual for Librarians

DIAN WALSTER

HOW-TO-DO-IT MANUALS FOR SCHOOL AND PUBLIC LIBRARIANS
Number 12

Series Editor: Barbara L. Stein

NEAL-SCHUMAN PUBLISHERS, INC.
New York, London

Published by Neal-Schuman Publishers, Inc.
100 Varick Street
New York, NY 10013

Printed and bound in the United States of America

Library of Congress Cataloging-in-Publication Data

Walster, Dian.
Managing time : a how-to-do-it manual for librarians / Dian Walster.
p. cm. — (How-to-do-it manuals for school and public librarians : no. 12)
Includes bibliographical references (p.) and index.
ISBN 1-55570-127-2
1. Libraries--Time management. 2. Library administration.
I. Title. II. Series.
Z682.35.T55W35 1993
025.1—dc20 93-4214
CIP

CONTENTS

PREFACE

First as a practicing librarian and then as a library educator, I was concerned that the tasks librarians need to accomplish are greater than the time available. There always seemed to be a discrepancy that created personal discomfort for librarians. This book, which began with my own need to balance time and effort as a librarian, grew as I learned about similar problems encountered by other librarians. It is my hope that *Managing Time: A How-To-Do-It Manual for Librarians* will help librarians choose time management techniques that improve both their personal and professional lives.

As a practicing librarian, I developed many of the methods and strategies expressed in this book. I did not read time management books or listen to time management tapes when I began. I did not have the time. By trial and error and adapting everyday wisdom (e.g., To Do lists, calendars, diaries) I discovered what worked for me. My original attempt at keeping a time diary was an extension of the personal journal writing I had learned as an English Composition and Creative Writing major. I extrapolated that if a personal diary was useful for attacking personal problems and issues, a professional diary could be equally useful for professional problems. Over the years the types of time diaries I kept varied in relation to the type of job I held and its complexity. The diary examples in this book are ideas that I have tried at one time or another. In fact, some of the examples in the text come directly from time diaries I kept as a high school library media specialist.

Another example of a personal issue represented in this book is the To Do list discussion. Hardly a novel approach to time management, the To Do list is a commonplace idea that has been around for years. Nevertheless, I never could make a To Do list work the way it was supposed to. Over years of trying different methods for keeping To Do lists, I discovered there were basic parameters in their construction. These are identified and analyzed. The range of ways to organize To Do lists comes from personal exploration with the different permutations described in this book.

I never planned on becoming a time management expert. I was content with exploring and trying out ideas to help me manage my library better. My first attempts at explaining successful time management to other librarians came from an awkward social moment. One day, at a district library media specialists' meeting, I was engaged in a friendly argument with another media specialist. We were trying to decide how the district had set up the equipment repair process. I said that at a meeting earlier in the year the budget officer had indicated that we could have equipment repaired in the district or we could request an outside bid. Although there were restrictions on the outside bidding process, I felt that the repair job I was thinking about required expertise not available within the district. My colleague said that all repairs had to be completed within the district. After discussing this for a few minutes, the other librarian said in exasperation, "Well, how do you know this is true? Do you keep records on everything you do and hear?" I said, "Yes!" and pulled out my time diary from the period in question. In it were my notes on the budget officer's speech. Of course, I could have misinterpreted the speech, but the other librarian was so intrigued with the time diary that the original question was forgotten. I explained how I created the diary, what kind of information I put in it, and how I found the time to do it. Later that year I presented the idea of the time diary to other librarians in the district. This was the beginning of my professional experience as a time management educator and consultant.

As I conducted more workshops and seminars about time management, I began to see a diversity of personalities among librarians and library staff. Librarians are not all the same. They approach and solve problems differently. Consequently, they need different time management strategies. I discovered I could no longer promote only my personally preferred methods for time management. I needed to extend the activities and techniques I recommended, and so I began a needs assessment on librarians and time management. This became the first step in an instructional design approach to time management for librarians. A more formal needs assessment based on personal interviews and focus groups indicated two major areas where time management was critical for librarians:

1. Librarians in school and small public libraries had needs not addressed in traditional time management materials.

2. Librarians had difficulty beginning time management and maintaining motivation once begun.

How does this book address the needs of librarians in all types of libraries?

The problems of librarians in large public and academic libraries are similar to middle managers in business environments. Most time management books address issues useful to librarians in larger organizations. In addition, librarians in larger organizations usually have recourse to professional development and collegial discussions with other professionals. Librarians in schools and small public libraries have unique problems. They may be isolated professionally, fulfill multiple roles, and have little access to professional development. This book was written specifically to include the needs of librarians in school and small public libraries. It provides examples from their environments and helps them create individualized professional development activities.

Is this book only for school librarians and librarians in small public libraries? Absolutely not! While the examples have been designed to meet the needs of a specific group, the general principles discussed in the book are useful for all librarians and meet the second need discussed above. To help translate the book more effectively into different settings, consider the following transformations when reading an example or idea:

- Instead of students you may wish to think about clients, patrons, or users.
- Look at the type of relationship that is presented. For example a librarian/library assistant relationship is an example of a supervisor/employee relationship, or a librarian/teacher relationship is an example of a peer relationship.
- Ignore the words that indicate a school or small public environment and think about the concepts expressed: a librarian picking up mail in a teacher's lounge could easily be a librarian picking up mail in a metropolitan library's mail room.

How does this book help librarians begin time management and maintain motivation?

Librarians in all environments—whether school, small public, large public, academic, or special libraries—can use the time management approach outlined in this book to begin time management and to maintain motivation over the long term. This system is not tied to a particular type of library. The system expressed in this book was created through two processes. The first was a review and analysis of current literature about time management. The second used an instructional design process to develop a method for helping librarians teach themselves about time management.

In reading the time management literature, I discovered a number of interesting patterns. Time management books fell into two basic categories:

1. Lists of time management techniques to apply or
2. An author's unique system of time management.

Some time management books focused on specific topics such as paper management, time styles, or energy cycles. Others were more general and looked at common time management problems such as: interruptions, meetings, and delegation. No single resource articulated the basic characteristics necessary for successful time management. In this book I identify five components that must be present in any system for time management to be successful:

- Motivation
- Self-awareness
- Analysis procedures
- Implementation techniques
- Planning strategies

These components create an overall framework for beginning time management and sustaining commitment over time. They can be used as criteria for analyzing a specific time management system or as the foundation for creating a personalized time management system. This taxonomy of time management components is a unique contribution to the literature of time management.

For this book the five components of time management were integrated into a self-instructional framework using instructional design principles. Knowing that there is a diversity of personality and approach among librarians, two types of self-instructional activities were designed. Specific recipes and day-to-day instructions for creating a time management system are included for librarians who look for more structured activities. Directions for librarians who prefer to create their own time management systems are also provided. In addition, beginning, intermediate, and advanced approaches to time management create a developmental sequence for gradually increasing time management knowledge and skills. This book addresses the issue of time management in a way no other book has done. It recognizes the need for diversity in choosing time management techniques, and it provides a method for librarians to move progressively from beginning to more advanced time management .

This book is the result of two scholarly processes. The first is an application of instructional design to creating a system for teaching librarians how to help themselves manage time. The second is an analysis of time management literature, since no single resource on time management provides a systematic process for choosing methods to meet individual needs. Many time management problems are created because librarians and library staff disagree on how a job should be completed, not because of lack of time. Personal differences may make librarians believe that one method is right and another wrong. Much time can be committed to arguing about the right way to do something. This belief in correct methods for using time is promoted by most classic time management systems. It can lower individual self-esteem and may inhibit effective time use. Therefore, the message of this book is: No time management technique is intrinsically right or wrong.

People are multidimensional and require complex as well as simple approaches to understanding and applying time management. They should make choices based on factors that provide personal satisfaction and increase professional growth. This book helps librarians make choices that are right for them as people and as part of a professional staff.

Author's Note: Case study examples in *Managing Time* apply equally to female and male librarians. For editorial convenience personal pronouns were randomly assigned. Readers may substitute he for she and she for he in all cases.

1 TIME MANAGEMENT AND LIBRARIANS

This chapter explores three aspects of librarians' time management:

- Time Challenges
- Positive Actions
- Creating a Personal System

Librarians face choices about how to use time effectively whether they work in public, special, or academic libraries or in school media centers. Responses to time problems may be easily identified. Irritation at the fourth telephone interruption when concentrating on budget figures would be readily identified as a time problem. Other time problems and responses are less apparent. Job dissatisfaction from perceptions of too much to do is less easily identified as a time problem. Guilt and frustration about not accomplishing goals may turn time pressures into significant problems. These may not only affect work performance but also home and personal life. Making decisions and taking actions to improve job satisfaction and personal achievement can be helped by understanding and managing time more effectively. Time management by itself is not an answer to all the problems faced by librarians. Time cannot be managed. Time is invariant. It is measured in seconds, minutes, hours, and days. It proceeds no matter how intense or efficient we are. Time cannot be changed, but behaviors, responses, choices, and ideas about time can be changed. Librarians can modify, reorganize, and reform their thinking about time to provide a happier, healthier, safer, and more satisfying work and personal environment.

The work of a librarian is complex, demanding, and in a state of constant change. It is also challenging and entertaining, and it leads to new awareness and understanding. Within this framework of ambiguity, innovation, and change, librarians make decisions. Priorities are created, time is allocated, and work is completed. The librarian's balance between what should be done and what is actually done is always in the red. Sufficient time and resources do not exist to complete all the tasks a librarian could undertake. This leads to frustration and sometimes anxiety and stress. Librarians work in a volatile and changing environment. It is necessary to have choices and techniques that can be applied to new and different situations. One size does not fit all in time management for librarians.

This book helps librarians understand the cycle of too much

to do and not enough time. It provides guidelines for making judgments that lead to professional excellence and greater personal satisfaction by reviewing a range of time management options. It proposes a process for choosing among alternatives. For readers who want concrete steps to follow, this book provides recipes that can be used directly. For readers who prefer more flexibility, this book offers a method for putting techniques together to meet personal needs. This book looks at ways to begin time management, at methods to implement new strategies, and at motivation to encourage long-term commitment. It helps librarians to be more successful at time management through self-awareness and self-esteem.

This chapter examines basic conflicts that create time challenges for librarians. Later chapters explore examples of resolutions to many of these time challenges. The theme for this book is *taking positive action in response to time challenges*. The book's concepts, activities, and recommendations are all based on creating a positive environment. In this chapter the broadest context for taking positive action is explored. Further chapters focus on specific situations and techniques. The overall purpose is to create a personal system for taking positive action in relationship to time management. The conclusion of this chapter establishes parameters for creating a time management system. Succeeding chapters provide the step-by-step details.

Six time challenges face librarians regularly:

- Role conflicts
- Establishing priorities
- Technology
- One-person libraries
- Organizational culture
- Routine challenges

TIME CHALLENGES

Understanding time challenges is the first step in successful time management. Librarians' job descriptions include both service and managerial responsibilities. These two activities can create time challenges through conflicting time needs. Establishing and maintaining priorities is another time challenge for librarians. Time-saving technologies such as telephones, computers, and media materials may actually add time challenges and must be evaluated carefully. Time challenges may vary with type of library. For example, one-person libraries are unique situations with unique time challenges. In schools, librarians at different grade levels face time challenges related to their students and the culture of the school.

Public librarians are also affected by the culture of their organization and their community. In addition, librarians must confront the routine time challenges of all managers: interruptions; conflicts in values with superiors, peers, and library users; paper management; and fluctuating energy levels. The next section describes each of these time challenges and discusses the implications for librarians' time management.

ROLE CONFLICTS BETWEEN SERVICE AND MANAGEMENT RESPONSIBILITIES

Librarians function in a highly complex and demanding work place. A librarian's responsibilities can be divided into two major categories: librarian as manager and librarian as service provider. The librarian as a manager creates and oversees budgets, supervises personnel, selects and evaluates materials, develops plans, and sets policy. The librarian as a service provider works in cooperation with teachers or library users, provides reference help, recommends reading, listening, or viewing materials, and creates and delivers instruction. These two functions result in different time values. The job of the manager is to plan, organize, and direct. It requires uninterrupted time for reflection, analysis, and creating priorities. The job of a service provider is to meet the needs of the library user. It requires the librarian to be available on demand. The conflicting requirements of the two jobs set up conflicting time choices for librarians.

Case of the Broken Projector

Consider the library media specialist who must complete budget figures and their justification for the next year. Two hours have been set aside on Tuesday afternoon to review the figures and write the justification statement. Because this activity was the highest priority for the day, no classes were scheduled into the library. Forty five minutes into the budget review, a distraught student bursts into the librarian's office: "My teacher sent me down. There's film all over the floor, and the teacher doesn't know what to do! We were just getting to the good part of the movie, too." The need for uninterrupted managerial time is in direct conflict with the user's need for a service provider available immediately. Whose need comes first? What would you want to do? What would you actually do?

One response would be to attend to the teacher's request for help. This is a need-based service demand. Taking care of the problem immediately is necessary for the class to continue. It probably will only take a few minutes to straighten out the film; then work on the budget can continue. The librarian decides to help the teacher, and 20 minutes later returns to continue work on the budget.

At the end of the two-hour block of time, minus the 20-minute interruption, only half the budget justification is completed. The librarian must now attend a scheduled meeting with the superintendent. Upon returning to the budget two days later, the librarian finds that it takes an hour to review the budget and reconstruct the justification argument. The two-hour task has now taken three hours or longer. In the interim, the librarian has also spent time worrying about not completing the budget and trying to schedule another time period for budget preparation.

The basic conflict between managerial time needs and service provider time demands was resolved by meeting the user need. Was the librarian right in meeting the immediate demand of the teacher and taking longer to complete the budget? Was this an effective use of time? Only the librarian in this situation can answer those questions. The good will derived from helping the teacher may balance the extra time spent on the budget. Nevertheless, a decision was made. The time challenge was to recognize the decision point—to make a reasoned judgment and not simply respond to a demand.

ESTABLISHING PRIORITIES

The conflict between the managerial and service functions of a librarian directly affects the time challenge of establishing priorities. The service function may be viewed as existing in the present; it is an ongoing and constant need. Managerial functions, particularly those of establishing priorities, exist as a need for the future. The time challenge is one of balancing short-term demands against long-term needs. The complexity of a librarian's job means that all possible activities cannot be completed. The librarian will make choices about the most important goals and objectives for the school or community, the librarian, library users, staff, students, parents, or community members. Once established, goals and objectives become priorities for activities accomplished in the short term and for planning that must occur for the long term. These in turn direct how time is managed and allocated to various library tasks.

Establishing priorities in a school library media center or a small public library is a much larger task than it initially appears. Priorities may be created for the library without reflection on personal needs and priorities. Priorities for work-related activities also need to be completed within the context of a professional's life as a whole. Librarians may integrate work-related goals and priorities with personal goals and priorities. If there are conflicts between personal priorities and values and those of the job, decisions must be made about which is more important. They should be conscious decisions; they should not be decisions made by default or failure to consider personal priorities in relationship to work priorities.

The time challenge to librarians in establishing priorities is to see multiple perspectives and then make choices about which course of action deserves precedence. Short-term and long-term needs will be considered. Personal and job-related issues will be examined. A balance will be established that results in both personal and work satisfaction.

TECHNOLOGICAL TIME CHALLENGES

Technology places unseen demands on time:

- Hidden time needs
- Instructional needs
- Maintenance needs

Technology adds layers of complexity to the job of a librarian. It serves to expand the overall library environment by opening avenues to multiple resources and materials not previously available. As technology widens access, it increases external pressures on the librarian. New technology brings time challenges related to different operating methods, instructional needs, and ongoing repair and maintenance. For each element of time saving implied by a technology there may be an equivalent time challenge.

The telephone is an example of a technology widely available in libraries. Even though many school and small public libraries do not have telephones, the pressure to add phone lines grows. Acquiring technologies such as data transmission computers and fax machines necessitates telephone lines. The telephone has expanded the range of resources for libraries. It provides immediate information about availability of materials from other sources. It saves personal search time. It has also increased time demands on the librarian. Telephone interruptions are one of the most frequently expressed time management problems. There is a widely held belief that a ringing telephone must be answered. The telephone is the ultimate demand device. Time savings from telephone technology are balanced with new time demands from the same technology.

A second time challenge accompanying new technologies is the need for education and instruction. Online public access catalogs (OPACs) are one example. Not only must the librarian learn to use the technology, but students, patrons, and other library users must also be instructed in its use. This need for instruction is both initial and ongoing. As new people begin to use the system, they must receive instruction. Once a basic card catalog was mastered, the essential skills could be transferred to almost any type of library or card catalog. The principles remained essentially the same. The same cannot be said for OPACs. Although some functions are fundamental across OPACs, many interactions vary based on the idiosyncrasies of a particular system.

The complexity of technology has increased the range of access to materials, but has also increased the time commitment necessary for creating informed users through instruction. Updates to card catalogs, such as the addition of new subject headings, were essentially clerical in nature. The basic structure of the card catalog and its use did not change. Updates in the technology of OPACs may require retraining for all staff and users. For example, the latest version of an OPAC screen changes the way information is organized. Instructions are given in a different order and include new possibilities for searching. Commands for accessing information have been altered and some options deleted. This requires users to learn and remember a new path through the system and new ways to access information. It will be confusing and frustrating until the updates have been mastered.

A third time challenge resulting from technology in libraries is the increased need for technical expertise and maintenance. While librarians seldom engage in actual repairs or maintenance, they must manage the process. It is one thing for a librarian to show an assistant how to clean a wand used for reading bar codes. It is another thing to know when to call and whom to call for a replacement wand to be sent by express courier. The breakdown of hardware and software may slow other operations and result in time expenditures higher than before the new technology was introduced. For example, a new bar code wand sent by regular mail might not arrive for two to five days. This could result in circulation being done by hand and then redone when the new wand arrives.

Investment of time for technology directly affects librarians. The major time challenge to librarians is the increased need to provide both managerial and instructional support related to the technologies. Instructional support must be measured both in the time needed to deliver training and the time needed by the librarian to read and keep up to date. To implement a new technology requires a major readjustment of priorities both in the short term and the long term.

TIME CHALLENGES FOR ONE-PERSON LIBRARIES

Librarians in one-person libraries are subjected to the maximum time challenge from the two roles of service provider and manager. They must be all things to all people. In addition, they serve as their own clerical staff. Therefore, it is critical to clearly understand why decisions are made. The librarian in the one-person library must be aware of the complexity of the position. Setting priorities is essential in the one-person library in order to function in all capacities successfully.

Using time management techniques and principles can help the librarian in the one-person library streamline routine, clerical, and managerial tasks. Time management cannot help librarians complete all possible tasks. They cannot all be done, no matter how efficient, effective, and responsible librarians are in their time management. This limitation must be accepted. The biggest time challenges to librarians in the one-person library are to establish reasonable expectations for themselves and to maintain positive self-esteem. Similarly, they must have appropriate expectations for the services the library can provide.

Case of Cooperative Checkout

For the past ten years Leslie has been the only librarian in a small public library. Leslie enjoyed the challenges and opportunities and found the library board and community to be cooperative and supportive. This year, Leslie wrote and received the library's first Library Services and Construction Act (LSCA) grant. Funds were awarded to purchase Spanish-language materials at all reading levels and to provide a children's story hour in Spanish. Leslie was both excited and concerned. The time needed to organize and manage the project would definitely cut into day-to-day library operations.

When the LSCA project was voted the number-one priority for the year by the board, Leslie was committed to finding the time to do the job well. After examining routine clerical and maintenance tasks, Leslie discovered that much time was spent assisting patrons with checkout. Consultations with board members, regular library users, and school librarians led Leslie to believe that most library users could complete a self-checkout process. With board approval, Leslie instituted self-checkout, intended to last until the LSCA project was implemented. A clear sign, in both Spanish and English, was designed and produced by the high school art department.

Although some library users, particularly young children, still needed assistance, most library users are capable and willing to participate in the new system. Overall, Leslie gained the time necessary to successfully manage the LSCA project. In addition, the self-checkout works so well that the board has agreed to continue the procedure indefinitely.

Organizational culture creates time challenges:

- Elementary schools
- Middle schools
- Junior high schools
- Senior high schools
- Public libraries

TIME AND ORGANIZATIONAL CULTURE

Librarians in both school and public libraries face time challenges resulting from the culture of the organization they work in. Organizations develop expectations over time of how managerial and service tasks will be accomplished. Library users expect consistent responses based on past experiences. Conflicts between organizational culture and personal expectations can result in time challenges for all librarians.

Working as a library media specialist in an elementary, middle school, junior high, or high school may result in time challenges unique to the culture of education. At each level the ages and abilities of students, the organizational style of the school, and the expectations of faculty, students, and staff will affect librarians' use of time. Although each school is unique, there are similarities between schools at various levels. These similarities may help librarians understand time management problems resulting from their own environment. Each of the time challenges identified for a specific grade level may be interesting to library media specialists at other levels. It may also be interesting to public librarians since understanding the problems of colleagues in different situations may place personal time challenges in perspective.

At the elementary level there may be smaller numbers in the overall student population. This often means less clerical staff and less support staff and greater reliance on the library media specialist to perform a wide range of jobs. The entering student population may be assumed to have negligible information skills and experience. There will also be a diversity of ability among the student population. The need for instructional activities and support is critical, and the greatest portion of an elementary library media specialist's time may be spent in direct instructional activities. The time challenge to elementary library media specialists is to establish other priorities around the need for direct instruction.

In the history of education, middle schools are a relatively recent addition. Consequently, there are fewer materials and guides specifically designed for the middle school population. Selection decisions must be made based on tools for the elementary, junior high, or high school. Information skills curricula may contain ambiguity about which skills belong at elementary, which at middle school level, and which at higher levels. There is also a need to identify student information skill levels and provide reinforcement and review if necessary. There are fewer materials specifically created for this mix of age and skills. The time challenge for middle school library media specialists is the need to consult the wide range of resources necessary to provide materials and activities for students and faculty. Since referring to multiple review sources may be necessary, middle school library media specialists must budget extra time for routine library tasks such as selection and curriculum development.

Junior high schools have many characteristics similar to senior high schools, and the time challenges presented in the senior high section below may also be applied to library media specialists at the junior high school level. Nevertheless, there is one characteristic unique to junior high schools that affects the library media specialist. Students at junior high school age have great social and emotional variability. They have a strong need for personal attention and guidance. This need is felt by both teachers and library media specialists. Teachers will have a greater need for materials to help students adjust to their changing physical and personal environment. Library media specialists will spend more time with students individually. The time challenge for junior high school library media specialists is to identify methods to cope with the greater emotional and social needs of the student population and the corresponding needs of the faculty.

The cultures of high schools will vary widely based on size and number of staff. Smaller high schools will more likely have homogeneity of philosophy and direction. Larger high schools will more likely contain subunits with implicit philosophies and directions. These sub-units may be in direct conflict with each other. In general, the organizational unit at the high school level has a greater probability of being a loosely connected structure. Each unit will have its own needs and priorities. There is a potential for strong philosophical differences among departments. The librarian may serve as a consultant and arbitrator for many issues.

The library media specialist at the high school level is more likely to be perceived as a manager rather than a teacher. Managerial responsibilities at the high school level also tend to be more complex. Budgets, collections, and range of supervisory responsibilities are usually greater. Decreased funding for schools has also lead to dramatic decreases in staffing of high school library media centers in the past years. Media centers that formerly had two or even three professional staff members may now be served by one library media specialist. The time challenge for each high school library media specialist is to identify clearly the role they wish to assume in their school's organizational structure. Clear objectives, priorities, and goals are essential at the high school level.

Librarians in public libraries must respond to the culture created by the community they serve. Time challenges may result from service and personal assistance expectations of library users and community members. In addition, the range of library users for the public librarian is both broad and deep. This requires extensive knowledge and personal communications skills, which can create further time challenges. Expectations of the community, the library board, and library users may also conflict with the personal or professional expectations of the librarian.

ROUTINE TIME CHALLENGES

People face similar and recurring time management challenges in all types of jobs and in their personal and professional lives. Four of the most prevalent are interruptions, values conflicts, paper management, and fluctuating energy levels. For librarians, each of these routine time challenges can be seen in the context of their professional role. Interruptions may reflect the basic conflict between the management and service roles of the librarian. Values conflicts may result from problems in establishing priorities that are clear to all interested parties. Paper management may be related both to establishing priorities and potential values conflicts. Fluctuating energy levels are directly related to understanding the relationship between personal life and work life.

Positive action results in three significant behavior changes:

Making satisfying choices
Developing proactive stances
Practicing assertiveness

TAKING POSITIVE ACTION

A goal of this book is to help librarians understand their responses to time challenges and to analyze the effectiveness of those responses. The next step is take positive action and, when necessary, change ineffective to effective responses. Focusing on personally satisfying choices, developing proactive behaviors, and practicing assertiveness techniques are three general approaches towards taking positive action. The next section provides an overview of how positive action results in effective time management. Chapters Two, Three, and Four describe specific techniques for getting started, for continuing time management effectiveness, and for planning for the future. Chapter Five shows how taking positive action can affect the integration of personal and professional priorities. Taking positive action toward managing library time challenges can lead to increased feelings of self-worth and self-esteem. It can also lead to a stronger library program that meets the current and future needs of users.

MAKING SATISFYING CHOICES

Choosing work activities that are interesting and believed to be valuable should result in feelings of job satisfaction. Why, then, do so many librarians seem dissatisfied with their jobs? Is it possible librarians are choosing tasks that are neither interesting nor intrinsically valuable? That does not seem likely. More likely, librarians are doing too many interesting and valuable activities, and are overwhelmed. When choosing from among an array of equally valuable activities it is possible to become dissatisfied with not being able to do them all. The seduction of time management is the fantasy that it creates an environment where all possible tasks can be accomplished. If this were true, time management would lead directly to personal and professional satisfaction. Unfortunately time management is not magic. The librarian will have to make choices from among interesting and valuable work activities. "The critical capability of the 1990s is controlling your life despite scores of tasks and activities competing for your attention" (Davidson 1991, 3). The challenge is to make choices that lead to personal and professional satisfaction.

One of the difficulties in achieving satisfaction is that different people are satisfied at different levels of completeness or accomplishment. For example, librarians who strive for outstanding levels of excellence in all tasks must complete activities with a high degree of proficiency to feel satisfied. Such librarians should consider reducing the number of their activities because "striving for perfection usually costs us more time than the increased benefits justify" (LeBoeuf 1979, 257). It takes more time to complete a task at a high-performance level. This means limiting the number of tasks. Librarians who require high levels of excellence will be more satisfied if they understand that they have a choice between the number of activities completed and the degree of perfection achieved. Conversely, librarians who are satisfied at lower levels of completeness or proficiency may conflict with peers or supervisors who feel differently. This conflict may serve to reduce feelings of satisfaction. Librarians who have less of a need for perfection will be more satisfied if they understand that they, too, have a choice between the number of activities completed and the degree of perfection achieved. The closer these decisions match the librarians' personal levels of satisfaction, the greater their feeling will be that they have managed their time appropriately.

When performing a task will not create satisfaction because of personal, professional, or temperamental opposition, carefully evaluate the options. Consider completing the task in minimum time. You want to "make the job simpler, eliminate waste and get maximum results with minimum effort" (Shapiro 1983, 40). Getting it over with might create the greatest satisfaction. Choose not to do the task if the consequences are oppressive. Continuing conflicts between personal beliefs and those of supervisors or peers means the job may not be appropriate. Organizations have varying personalities and priorities. It may be necessary to change jobs or locations to maintain personal and professional well being. Consider balancing the desires and demands of others with your own personal levels of satisfaction in completing those tasks. As satisfaction decreases, so does enthusiasm, energy, and ability to complete tasks. There will be conflicts in any situation of intense interpersonal cooperation and communication. However, understanding personal needs and satisfaction levels makes it easier to understand and work with others.

An initial step in creating personal and professional satisfaction is to clearly understand what is satisfying to you. What makes you feel good? What do you do that leaves you with the belief that you have made a difference? Complete Exercise 1 to

TIME MANAGEMENT EXERCISE 1

Personal Satisfaction—20 minutes

1. Find a quiet space and take a watch, a pencil and a time management notebook.
2. Take two minutes and write as many answers as come to mind for the following question: What did I do in the past week that made me feel satisfied and happy?
3. Concentrate only on positive activities that were rewarding to you personally. Do not limit your answers to work related activities. Review your answers in two minutes and add any comments you wish.
4. Take two more minutes and write as many answers as come to mind for the following question: What did I do in the past six months that made me feel satisfied and happy?
5. Concentrate only on positive activities that were rewarding to you personally. Do not limit your list to work related activities. Review your answers in two minutes and add any comments you wish.
6. Take two minutes and write as many answers as come to mind for the following question: What would I like to do in the future that would make me happy and satisfied?
7. Concentrate on positive activities that are rewarding to you personally. Do not limit your list to work related activities. Review your answers in two minutes and add any comments you wish.
8. Review your lists of activities for the past. Identify two characteristics that made you feel satisfied and happy.
9. Review your list of activities for the future. Are there activities which match the characteristics of past activities which made you satisfied and happy? Make that activity a priority and try it out this week.

help identify activities that are satisfying to you. Use the results of this exercise when making decisions about tasks or activities.

DEVELOPING PROACTIVE BEHAVIORS

Deciding which activities offer feelings of personal and

professional satisfaction opens up ways for promoting ideas and beliefs to other people. Taking positive action by developing proactive behaviors helps reinforce satisfying choices. Proactive behavior involves creating direction, anticipating problems, and planning for the future. Proaction is a positive approach. It gives one a feeling of control. A proactive stance is not always comfortable, but there is usually a feeling of positive direction and accomplishment. There is also the possibility of making goals, objectives, and outcomes clearer to other people and thus increasing both material and emotional support for programs and people. Proactive behavior leads to greater feelings of self-worth because librarians are making choices that fit with personal beliefs about how libraries should function. It can be a way to create consensus and community feeling for the library and its programs.

Planning, information dissemination and communication, encouraging positive feelings, practicing assertiveness, and evaluating library programs are all proactive behaviors. Each has an implication for responding to library time challenges. Planning is directly related to the time challenge of establishing priorities. Appropriate planning can help involve others in the establishment of library priorities and reduce the time needed to create consensus. Disseminating information and improving communication can be helpful in the time challenges of technology and the conflicts between the managerial and service provider roles. In each case, more informed library users will make it easier for librarians to explain choices that result in conflicts. Encouraging positive feelings toward libraries and librarians can be effective in minimizing routine time challenges such as interruptions, values conflicts, and external deadlines. Assertive behavior is invaluable in dealing with all time challenges and will be discussed in detail below. Evaluating the library program can identify time challenges for special circumstances and varying types of libraries. Specific instances of proactive behavior by librarians include:

- Communicating expectations for scheduling, requesting library materials, facilities, and services that require coordination.
- Serving on planning committees in order to know in advance what library materials will be needed.
- Asking for regular reports or scheduling informational meetings with key committee members.

- Stating goals, objectives, and long-range and short-range plans, and involving school or community members in their creation.
- Disseminating information and creating positive attitudes on a regular basis—not only when money, resources, or assistance is needed.
- Giving recognition to people who help.
- Promoting the library program before a crisis appears.
- Evaluating trends that might adversely affect the library.
- Attending to the outside environment and internal changes in school or community policies and procedures that will influence the library.
- Knowing about potential changes in policies or procedures to predict planning needs and possibilities for positive responses.
- Focusing on activities and strategies that demonstrate strength rather than weaknesses.
- Concentrating on maintaining strengths and improving weaknesses.
- Realistically examining school or community impressions of the library and creating public relations activities to reinforce positive impressions and improve negative impressions.
- Developing and disseminating planning documents such as a collection development plan, an information skills curriculum, or a handicapped access process.

PRACTICING ASSERTIVENESS

Assertiveness is a specific type of a proactive behavior for coping with conflicts resulting from the time challenges of librarians. Practicing assertiveness also aids in following through with proactive behavior. For example, the conflicting roles of manager and service provider mean that at some point librarians need to clearly state that they cannot immediately respond to a library users demand. Practicing assertive behavior can resolve the conflict between the need for uninterrupted time to reflect and the need to provide service. As one researcher has stated, assertive behavior "increases a librarian's sense of self-esteem for having taken positive, realistic action in an appropriate and considerate manner, and it may bring a wide variety of positive resolutions to conflicts." (Caputo 1984, 19).

An excellent way of practicing assertiveness is to identify

examples of reactive behaviors and assertively turn them into proactive behaviors. People who react are trying to put out others' fires. They are responding to external pressures and demands. Reacting can lead to feeling a lack of control. It can also lead to anger, anxiety, frustration, lack of incentive, and many other negative emotions and feelings. Constantly reacting to requests may result in a lack of direction or identity.

Turning reactive behaviors into assertive behaviors means applying techniques such as those suggested by Janette Caputo in *The Assertive Librarian* (1984). Two problems librarians face in making assertive statements are saying no and setting limits. In the example below there are assertive *no* statements and statements that set limits on the problem. As you read the situation described below, consider the suggested assertive statements. Create your own assertive *no* statements and assertive statements setting limits for the example. Compare your responses with the samples provided. Following the example is an exercise for practicing assertive *no* statements and statements setting limits. Practice is the key to implementing more assertive behavior and improving time management.

Case of the Interrupted Search

A student rushes into the library and interrupts you in the middle of a database search while you are looking for articles on how to teach search strategies for the CD-ROM. "I need a book right now to read in my history class. I forgot to get one and the teacher will be really angry." You leave the terminal and help the student find a book. When you return, the software has turned itself off; your descriptors are lost, and you must begin the search again.

Assertive *No* Statements

- No, I cannot help you right now. I am working on a project that I must finish.
- No, I cannot help you find a book. I must finish this search first.
- No, I cannot help you.

Assertive Statements Setting Limits

- I will help you this time, but next time you will need to ask at least ten minutes before class begins.
- I will be available to help you in 15 minutes. Get a pass from your teacher to return to the library then.

- I will help you this time, but next time bring your class reading list with you.

Saying *no* and making statements setting limits are two effective ways of improving use of time. *No* statements indicate specifically what you are unwilling to do. You may or may not include explanations. As you begin to make more *no* statements, you will be taken more seriously. Colleagues, students, and library users will become aware that you really

TIME MANAGEMENT EXERCISE 2

Practicing Assertive Statements—35 minutes

1. In two minutes write down as many situations as you can think of where you engaged in reactive behavior. Examples could include being interrupted while eating lunch, responding automatically to a ringing telephone, etc.
2. Choose one situation and write three *no* statements and three assertive statements setting limits that you could use. Review your statements.
3. Imagine yourself in the situation above. Practice making an assertive *no* statement or a statement setting limits that you wrote down. How does the other person react? Imagine how you would respond.
4. Repeat this process by visualizing different people and different situations. Practice in a nonthreatening environment, such as your imagination, is an excellent method of increasing assertive behavior.
5. Ask a person you trust to take the part of a student, library user or coworker. Practice assertive *no* statements or assertive statements setting limits.
6. As a further exercise think of a situation that occurred recently where you could have used an assertive statement. Replay the situation in your mind and respond with an assertive *no* statement or a statement setting limits. Try to imagine the response of the other person.
7. In the next two days make an assertive *no* statement or a statement setting limits. Reward yourself with a *well done* statement.

mean *no* because you continue to stand firm. They will also begin to realize that when you say *yes* you can be counted on to be interested and enthusiastic about the task. When you make assertive statements setting limits and follow through with corresponding behavior similar positive results will occur.

Successful time management systems contain five basic components:

Motivation
Self awareness
Analysis procedures
Implementation techniques
Planning strategies

CREATING A TIME MANAGEMENT SYSTEM

This book provides a guide to creating and implementing a time management system. Each person has differing needs, goals, and styles. It is important to create a time management system that reflects your personality and preferred style. The wrong plan may be physically possible, but certainly not optimally useful. In developing a time management system for yourself, make choices that result both in effective use of time and personal comfort. Choosing time strategies that work with your natural inclination will result in the greatest rewards. Creating a time management system requires five basic components: motivation, self awareness, analysis procedures, implementation techniques, and planning strategies. In this chapter, the five components will be defined and their relationships discussed. The following chapters explore methods for integrating these components into time management systems from the simple to complex. The final chapter looks at the effects of time management on the librarian's professional and personal life. Throughout the book, exercises and examples are provided to demonstrate how time decisions are made and to allow the opportunity to practice making time decisions.

MOTIVATION

Motivation is the first component of a time management system. It consists of both internal and external factors. Generally the process of time management begins with strong internal motivation to make changes. Over time, motivation may decrease or even disappear. The motivation component of your time management system will help you to uncover both conscious and unconscious forces that make you want to manage time more effectively. It provides a method to feed the strong feelings that led you to examine time management. Internal motivation and internal needs will change over time. Monitoring motivation and looking for activities or materials that help maintain and increase motivation are critical.

External elements, such as the response of others to changes, also affect one's commitment to time management. Ongoing support helps one to make changes, even if they are difficult. Distinguishing between supportive and unsupportive people and developing a mechanism for continuing support contribute to motivation.

SELF-AWARENESS

Matching time management strategies with personal preferences will help you to realize which aspects of self-awareness have the greatest impact on time management. Your relationship to time, your relationship to the environment and its organization, and your self-esteem are the three major areas of self-awareness discussed in this book. Understanding how you use time and organize space and how comfortable you are with making changes smoothes the time management transition. By increasing awareness of preferences and dislikes in each area, you increase the probability of success with time management.

Each of us responds to and uses time differently. Some people are almost always early for appointments; some people are almost always late for appointments. This is a simple example of consistent, personal response to time. More complex relationships to time include waiting until the last minute to complete projects, attending to the details but not the overall picture, attending to the overall picture but not the details, difficulty in delegating or reassigning responsibilities, and wanting to complete projects perfectly. When you have a picture of the ways in which you consistently relate to time, you can start choosing techniques and strategies that capitalize on your natural style.

Just as librarians have a relationship to time, they also have a personal relationship to the environment and its organization. We all know people whose desks are piled so high with paper that it is difficult to believe they can ever find anything. If asked for something, however, they might reply, "Oh, I know right where that is!" Another type is the person who has a completely clear desk. The silent question asked about this person might be, "Do they really do any work?" These are examples of a relationship to the physical environment and its organization. Some people prefer things out and visible; others prefer them put away in drawers and cabinets. Creating a paper management system that is not in synchronization with a librarian's preferred use of space may lead to greater confusion and dissatisfaction than the original problem.

Self-esteem is a critical component to success in any endeavor, but particularly in time management. Self-esteem will help you understand that the way you relate to time and the environment is appropriate. Differences are acceptable and to be expected. The self-awareness component of your time management system will help you to create a system that reflects your personality and natural inclinations. Self-esteem and the ability to take risks are interdependent. Changing your behavior and actions to improve time management does involve risk taking. Being aware of your level of self-esteem and your level of risk taking can improve your chances for being successful in managing your time.

ANALYSIS PROCEDURES

Analysis procedures provide concrete and specific methods for evaluating your use of time. Analysis procedures range from simple internal dialogues and choices to complex computer programs. They help identify personal preferences, goals, objectives, and priorities. They provide the raw material for a time management system, but they must be chosen with care and precision. An analysis procedure that does not reflect and support personal preferences can decrease motivation, reducing effectiveness and interest in time management. Although many books and consultants on time management advocate their own analysis method as the only model for success, no one approach can be successful for all people. Nor will any one method be continually successful for the same person. The motivation gained through a single analysis procedure will wane after a period. Variety is necessary. Motivation level, experience with time management, and personal goals will dictate which choices are appropriate under which conditions.

IMPLEMENTATION TECHNIQUES

The implementation stage of a time management system is the application of time management techniques—the things you do to change your actions and behaviors. Time management techniques may be simple or complex, long term or short term, visible or invisible, and result in major or minor alterations in your behavior and the behavior of those around you. In choosing and implementing a time management technique, it is important to look at the dimensions of the technique and the consequences of implementation. This may help you avoid negative consequences and look forward to positive consequences. It is a way of reducing risk. Either minimizing negative consequences or maximizing positive consequences results in an increase in motivation.

Time management techniques are the basis for most books on time management, and many time management books have good ideas, exercises, and activities (Harris 1985; Haynes 1987; Hobbs 1987; Januz 1981; Lebov 1980; Mackenzie and Waldo 1981; Seivert 1989; Silcox 1980; Winston 1983). At least they will be effective for someone, if not for you. Your responsibility is to discover, through practice and observation, which techniques work best for you. With the wide range of techniques available, you will need to be selective. Discard those that do not work for you and those that seem boring or difficult. Concentrate on choosing techniques and activities that are fun and satisfying. Just as some tennis players are known for their two-handed backhand or their overhead lob, you can concentrate on the excellence of your To Do List or your Interruption Eliminator technique. If a technique does not result in personal comfort, look for one that does and make use of it. The range of possible implementation techniques is almost limitless.

Everyone uses such time management techniques as To Do lists, calendars, appointment books, address files, and "urgent" folders. Many people read a new time management book because current techniques are not working. They may have become stale or uninteresting, or actually hinder efficiency or effectiveness. The following exercise helps to identify time management techniques you already use while providing a method to examine their usefulness. It is the beginning of your personal time management system. In the next chapter you will use this information as a step in beginning time management.

PLANNING STRATEGIES

The final component in creating a time management system is a range of planning strategies. Planning is the process by which goals and objectives are established and methods of implementation evaluated and put in place. Analysis provides the information, techniques provide the methods, but planning provides the reason, the motivation, and the possible

TIME MANAGEMENT EXERCISE 3

Current Implementation Techniques—10 minutes

1. In three minutes write down the time management techniques you use. They can be as simple as setting your watch ahead five minutes or as complex as a computer notebook which keeps your schedule.
2. Write down anything you do that relates to time or planning.
3. In two minutes review your list and add comments.
4. Star the three techniques you think are most effective.
5. Star the three techniques you use most often.
6. Are four and five the same items? If not, why not?
7. Keep this list on hand as you proceed through the book. Use it to help create a list of time management techniques that are easy for you to use and that are effective.

results. There are many ways to plan and many possible levels on which to engage in planning activity, from the strategic to the tactical, the short term to the long term. It is important to make choices from among the available options that support your personal preferences and needs.

Use this book to take positive action in response to your time challenges!

A LOOK AHEAD

Each of the five components discussed above is part of a complete time management system: motivation, self awareness, analysis procedures, implementation techniques, and planning strategies. The next three chapters look in detail at the five components and provide suggestions for making choices among the many alternatives. Chapter Two leads you step by step through a process to begin creating a time management system. It helps you focus on simple and easily accomplished activities. Chapter Three looks at more advanced time management techniques and activities. It develops procedures for complex analysis and provides ways to translate from knowing to doing. Chapter Four focuses on creating planning strategies and increasing self-esteem. It helps you develop a system to balance work and personal goals.

Exercises and examples are provided to aid time management. Examples present a wide range of time management styles and preferences. You may not always see yourself in the example. If you do not, consider if the person reminds you of a peer, supervisor, or family member. Even though the example may not be relevant to you, perhaps you can learn something about how other people solve time management problems. Use these examples to help you relate to people with different styles and preferences. Complete those exercises that appear to be interesting, or of possible value. Do not feel obligated to engage in every exercise as it appears in the book. Later you may return to and use an exercise when it becomes necessary to solve a particular problem you encounter.

As you read through the next three chapters, begin to identify examples and methods that reflect your feelings and beliefs. Jot down in a notebook those you feel most strongly about or keep an audio or video tape record. This list will eventually become part of your personal time management system. These new activities can be compared to the time management techniques you already use and the list you compiled in Exercise 3. In your notebook, audio, or video record, also include details of motivational activities, personal style preferences, analysis procedures, time management techniques, and planning strategies you have tried. Highlight those you find most satisfying. Make notations on ideas which did not work and guesses about why. Keep a record of what works and what does not work. This helps you reflect on and improve your time management. Refer to the bibliography for further materials to provide depth and breadth to your knowledge of time management.

2 GETTING STARTED

Getting Started with time management involves:

- Committing to change
- Understanding time use
- Using simple analyses
- Trying new techniques
- Beginning to plan

There are methods to begin time management that take a minimum amount of time and result in immediate success. This chapter discusses simple approaches to beginning time management. Throughout the chapter, time management exercises help librarians choose activities to match their personal preferences and needs. The five components of a time management system are explored to provide the foundation for creating an effective plan. The first topic is initial motivation: how it is generated and how it may be drawn on to increase effectiveness. Self-awareness of time use is explored, and librarians with different approaches to time are described. Time-out techniques, a simple time diary, reflective evaluation, and activities checklists represent a range of analysis procedures for the time management beginner. Implementation techniques related to creating To Do lists and managing interruptions are examined. Planning is discussed in terms of prioritizing activities and three simple ways of beginning to plan are reviewed. Finally, organizing the five components into a simple system for the beginning time manager is discussed.

COMMITMENT TO CHANGE

How do you get started with time management? Getting started implies making a commitment to change. Because you have chosen to read this book on time management, you have taken the first step towards a commitment to change. You are motivated and believe that something different needs to be done. You are committed to understanding and relating to time in a different way. This commitment can change what you do and how you act. To energize this commitment, plan activities that result in success. As beginning projects, choose short activities that can be reasonably accomplished. The following exercise leads to immediate success. It requires a pad of paper, a pen, and a clock or a watch. After completing the exercise, you will know more about yourself, your situa-

TIME MANAGEMENT EXERCISE 4

Making a Commitment—15 minutes

1. On the top of a piece of clean new paper or in your time management notebook, write down one time problem you would like to resolve.
2. Choose only *one* problem. Start small and be realistic. Try to use no more than 25 words to state the problem.
3. Sit quietly for a minute and think. What could you do to change the situation? Consider your behavior, the behavior of others, environmental changes, etc.
4. In two minutes, list as many ideas as you can think of to improve the situation. Do not worry if they seem impractical or difficult to do. Try to create a wide variety of ways to solve the problem. Be creative.
5. Reread the list and circle the two solutions which you believe have the greatest likelihood of success.
6. Commit to implementing one solution immediately. Give the idea a reasonable trial. If it does not seem to be working, try the second idea. Take action and make a commitment towards improved time management.
7. Keep notes (either mental or written) on what worked and what did not. Your success is in *trying* to make a change. No matter what the actual outcome you will have learned.

tion, and controlling time. Making this initial commitment is a strong indication that things are improving.

HOW LIBRARIANS USE TIME

Commitment to change does not need to be uncomfortable or difficult. Although trying new activities may require more intense concentration, new behaviors, techniques, and strategies that fit with your personality and preferences will be more comfortable. How do you choose a time management strategy that complements your personal preferences? If you like working with broad concepts and strategies, evaluate the detail level of the time management activity. Choose activities that are less detail oriented. If you require extensive background information before making a decision, be certain to budget time for information gathering in your decision making process. If you like working on multiple projects simultaneously, consider carefully projects which require intensive and continuous time commitment. Managing time is difficult enough without trying to alter your basic identity at the same time. The three examples provided above parallel three dimensions of time use: thinking preferences, decision making preferences, and work style preferences. This section covers opposite ends of each of the three dimensions, providing six different profiles of how librarians use time.

Conceptualizers and organizers represent the opposite ends of the thinking preferences dimension. Conceptualizers see the overall picture and like to understand how all the pieces fit together. They are not interested in details; in fact, details can become obstacles to them. Organizers, on the other hand, thrive on details. They enjoy filing, sorting and categorizing. Finding the precisely correct place for each idea or item is part of what an organizer prefers to do.

Decision making preferences fall into the information gatherer and risk taker categories. Information gatherers are concerned about making appropriate decisions. They want to collect as much information as possible before making a decision. This often leads them to make no decision because sufficient information is not available. In counterpoint, risk takers are quite willing to make decisions with little or no information. They like life to be exciting and will often wait until the final moments and complete a project in a rush of activity.

At first glance the names multitasker and achiever may not appear to represent opposite preferences for work styles. However, the multitasker likes to work on many projects simultaneously. Variety and change are important to the multitasker. Completing tasks takes a secondary position. The achiever, on the other hand, is more likely to work on one project at a time focusing on doing an excellent job. Achievers want to complete everything perfectly; regardless of its importance. This focus on perfection can inhibit the achiever from successful completion of tasks and increase the time expended.

The author's work with librarians across the country yielded the observation that no one way of using time predominates. Although the profession is often seen by others as composed predominantly of organizers or achievers, this is not the reality. All the time use preferences suggested above are as applicable to librarians as they are to people in general.

Presented below are descriptions of librarians that depict the six time use preferences discussed. As you read through a description of each librarian's activities, make a guess about which time use preference is represented.

Case of the Harried Librarian

Pat

Upon entering the library Tuesday morning, Pat headed for the circulation desk to pick up the quarterly circulation statistics. In order for the library to be eligible for a special grant of $1000, proof of increased circulation was due to the State Library by four that afternoon. While at the desk, an elderly patron asked Pat to set up a microfiche reader for viewing genealogy material. In order to help the patron, Pat left the circulation desk without picking up the statistics.

On the way to the library office a headline in the daily newspaper caught Pat's eye. The lead story would be perfect for a new display the library was completing on adult literacy programs in the area. Pat immediately went to the photocopier and turned it on. While it warmed up, Pat remembered that copies also needed to be made of the new book list. Going into the office to get the bibliography originals, he stepped into a pool of water from a leaky window. After setting the newspaper on the desk, he looked up the city maintenance number.

While waiting for the maintenance department to answer the phone, Pat glanced at the Tuesday schedule. The Book Discussion Club was meeting was in ten minutes! The club's agenda for today was to set the reading list for the next six months. Pat could not miss the meeting. In the middle of the book discussion meeting, an irritated patron interrupted: "I can't find today's paper! What happened to it?" Pat retrieved the paper from the library office, gave it to the patron and returned to the book discussion meeting.

By the end of the day, Pat was exhausted and staring at an empty computer screen headed "Book Discussion Reading List." The circulation statistics were late; the window still leaked; and someone had torn the article on the new literacy program out of the paper.

Psychologists call this type of activity "fuguing," moving from one task to the next and never quite completing anything. This is an example of a multitasker's use of time. The basic problem is that tasks do not get completed. Presented below is another look at Pat's day. Techniques of particular value to multitaskers are used to increase task completion and minimize distractions.

After reading an article on time preferences, Pat decided that, for a Multitasker, his first priority is to begin each day with a minimum of distractions. Every morning Pat goes into the library office, closes the door, and reviews the daily schedule of activities. Anyone or anything that threatens to interrupt this routine is rerouted. If a member of the Friends group caught Pat in the parking lot and asked to have the reading list for the book discussion changed, Pat's response might now be, "Please write down the details and leave them on the circulation desk. I will review them and call you back by 3:00 p.m." Establishing specific times for dealing with activities is useful to a multitasker. Pat might even set an alarm clock or watch to ring at 3:00 p.m. each day as a reminder to review and return phone calls and messages.

Pat enjoys working on many tasks simultaneously, but realizes it may not be an effective behavior for all occasions. Consequently, he has established Friday afternoons as multitasking time. During this period, he goes from task to task as the mood or interests dictate. The important difference is that at least two of the tasks begun on a Friday afternoon must also be completed that Friday afternoon. They may be small items such as putting a letter in the mail or returning a phone call. This gives Pat the satisfaction of working on many different things, but also completing specific activities and generally feeling more satisfied.

Pat changed by slowing down and thinking about how to complete tasks more effectively. Distractions were eliminated as much as possible. Pat also found ways to work on multiple activities and retain the satisfaction of a preferred time use method.

Case of the Clashing Classes

Dana

Dana began the day early by redoing the plastic jackets put on the new books by parent volunteers yesterday. Several of the plastic jackets were crooked and improperly taped. At 7:30 a.m., Jerry, the library aide, arrived and began to check the cards that had been filed above the rod in the card catalog by parent volunteers. When Jerry finished, the cards were still above the rod because Dana wanted to review them to be certain they were correctly filed. First period, due to an unexpected teacher illness, two classes arrived in the library. One was scheduled to begin research work with their teacher on countries of the world. The other was a first-grade class accompanied by a teacher's aide who needed to return to the second-grade classroom immediately. A substitute teacher for the first-grade class was scheduled to arrive within an hour.

This particular first-grade class required close supervision. They generally responded well to being read to, but could be out of control when left on their own. Dana was in a dilemma. An intensive instructional session and worksheet activity had been prepared for the research class. The activity needed proper explanation and students had to be shown the appropriate way to find information. Dana did not believe the teacher could deliver the lesson completely and accurately. On the other hand, Jerry might not be able to keep the attention of the first grade class, which then might become noisy or difficult. Dana decided that Jerry should read to the first grade class, but she chose the books to be read. Because she was not happy with Jerry reading to the first graders, Dana interrupted the prepared research lesson to check on Jerry regularly.

At the end of the day Dana was exhausted and unsatisfied. The shelving done by parent volunteers needed to be checked, but Dana was just too tired. She decided to arrive even earlier the next morning and come in on the weekend for a few hours to catch up.

Dana is an achiever. Like the multitasker, the achiever may have problems completing tasks, but for different reasons. Even when a job is finished, the achiever may not always be satisfied. Presented below is Dana's day incorporating some activities and techniques that can help an achiever distinguish between reasonable and unreasonable expectations.

Dana wants to have more family time and not feel so tired at the end of the day. The first time management strategy that Dana decides to try out is examining the need to correct what parent volunteers have done. Dana, who has successfully learned to delegate some tasks to the parent volunteers, now decides that it is time to leave the follow-through to the volunteers. Dana will no longer check and double check jobs done by parent volunteers. Some tasks will not be completed perfectly, but Dana can now arrive at school at the normal starting time. Dana has decided that most clerical tasks are not top priority items and can be done adequately but not necessarily perfectly.

When a first-grade class arrives in the library unexpectedly, Dana now realizes that two choices are possible. The class does not have to be accepted. Dana can say, "No, it is not possible to take the first grade class at this time. Another class has been scheduled into the library." Another choice is to have

Jerry read to the students, select the books, and carry through with all responsibilities. Dana does not need to interrupt the research lesson to check on Jerry. Dana may concentrate on completing the research lesson and leave the first graders to Jerry. This leaves both Jerry and Dana feeling more satisfied and comfortable. In fact, they decide to relax and have a cup of coffee together later that morning. Jerry feels good because Dana delegated responsibility and left it to Jerry to carry out the assignments. Dana feels good because the students really seemed interested in the research project.

Terry

Case of the Possibly Postponed Puppets

Terry was sitting at table in the library reviewing the information skills curriculum for the school. Suddenly, a third-grade class appeared at the front door of the library. From the back door of the library, a kindergarten class trooped in. Terry thought the library was unscheduled. "Don't you remember? I talked to you in the lunch room last week about bringing my class in to use the new CD-ROM encyclopedia," said the third-grade teacher. The kindergarten teacher was settling the students into the reading pit, obviously preparing them for some type of activity. Upon questioning, Terry discovered they were ready for a puppet show on the real story of the three little pigs by A. Wolfe. This had been planned at the beginning of the year as part of a series of monthly puppet shows to be held on the third Thursday of each month. Terry thought frantically. It would be impossible to do both classes at the same time. Just as Terry was about to ask the third-grade teacher, who had minimal experience, to begin the CD-ROM lesson, the principal stepped into the library. "The library budget was due two days ago. I have left two messages asking if you needed extra time. What are you planning on doing?" Terry was overwhelmed by the problems created from not paying attention to details.

The day-to-day, clerical, and detail-oriented tasks such as returning phone calls and following up on commitments are difficult for a conceptualizer such as Terry. Finding energy is not a problem for these people, but organization is a problem. Routine tasks slow them down. Presented below is an example of Terry's day incorporating strategies and activities that are useful for people with the conceptualizer time use preference.

Terry has had too many days full of unexpected things happening because appointments and deadlines were forgotten. At a time management workshop Terry discovered a simple system to schedule classes into the library. A large wall chart has been placed in the library workroom that covers one month of library time. Teachers are responsible for filling in the appropriate days and times when their classes will be in the library with a brief notation about the topic. If a teacher discovers a time conflict, then Terry is consulted. For the most part, teachers are happy about this arrangement. Terry is ready when their classes arrive, and they can see how busy the library is. Terry has asked for help with the details of scheduling classes, and the teachers have willingly complied.

Another activity Terry has implemented is a simple routine to minimize forgetting. Terry never seemed to find the time to respond to phone calls. It was a continuous and chronic problem mostly because the content of phone calls was forgotten almost as soon as Terry hung up the phone. Even when Terry did take notes on phone calls, they were on scraps of paper soon lost or discarded. Terry now takes all phone messages on chartreuse colored message pads with a space for name, phone number, and message. Each of these areas is routinely filled in for each phone call. When the call is completed, Terry quickly notes on the bottom if this is an urgent problem. Urgent problems are placed in one stack, all other phone messages in another. At the same time each day, Terry looks at the Urgent phone messages and completes the necessary activities. Other phone calls are returned or taken care on Tuesday or Thursday morning. The notes are seldom lost because of their color, and they usually contain sufficient information for follow-through to needed actions.

Case of Delayed Automation

Chris

In January, the library board allocated Chris an impressive budget to automate the circulation and catalog systems. Due to budgeting constraints and priorities, it was necessary to expend the money by December 30th. Chris began the year by gathering information about all the types of automated systems None of them seemed to exactly fit the needs of the library. The papers, brochures, and information went into a file. Chris was going to think about it until June. In early June, the Chair of the library board dropped by Chris's office. A new automation system had been demonstrated at a national library board conference. It was wonderful. Chris should seriously consider purchasing it.

Chris had already looked at the system. Even though the board Chair thought it was good, it lacked two important features the library really needed. Chris became swamped with the summer reading program, and then it was the middle of August. At the end of August one of the major library companies was introducing a new automation system for small libraries. Chris decided to delay choosing a system until this new and improved product was available. There were production delays in the new system, and a prototype was not available until the middle of September. When Chris finally saw the system demonstrated on October 27th, it was not at all what the library needed. In order for the paperwork to be properly managed and payment made by December 30th, Chris needed to order a system by November 15th. Chris narrowed the choices down to two from the products researched earlier in the year. Upon further inquiries, it was discovered that one company had gone out of business and the other had increased its prices by 35 percent. Chris was in a dilemma. No system was exactly right. It would be impossible to satisfy everyone. Chris was discouraged and unhappy.

Chris is an information gatherer. Librarians like Chris are in a decision making dilemma. They are always concerned about whether or not their decisions will be correct. In this respect they are much like achievers. However, an achiever will often complete a task even though not completely satisfied. An information gatherer will leave things to chance rather than make a wrong decision. Presented below is a sample of ways in which Chris could enhance time management through improved decision making.

Chris knew that choosing an automation system was going to be difficult. It was a lot of money to spend, and it did not look as if any system was going to be flawless. Chris decided to make the choice by developing a timeline with reverse chronology. Since the funds had to be expended by December 30th, Chris worked backward from this time to create dates for interim decisions. This would break the large decision of choosing an automation system into a set of smaller components. By doing this, Chris discovered that the first task was to outline the priorities and needs of the library and community. Chris gathered this information from board members, library users, library volunteers, staff members, and the general community.

Chris then realized it was impossible to satisfy everyone. Rather than letting this fact paralyze the decision making process, Chris decided to make a list of what could happen if an unpopular choice was made. After identifying and examining the fears, Chris found that the overall decision did not appear so difficult. Whatever new automation system was chosen would meet a majority of the library's requirements. A strong case could be made for a final decision based on needs and priorities.

After carefully considering the alternatives and making these smaller decisions during the year, Chris put in an order for the new automation system in June. During the summer reading program, Chris was able to relax and enjoy the excitement because the year's large decision had been completed successfully.

Case of the Rewritten Grant

Alex

It was Friday afternoon at 3:30 p.m. Alex had been told that if the school's revised grant proposal was received by 5 p.m. the school was assured of receiving significant funding for renovating the library media center. Alex had been given a month to make the revisions requested by the grant committee, but they seemed minor. It would only take a few minutes to put the changes into the computer and print out a new version. As Alex started the revisions, it was clear that the justification section needed to be completely rewritten. The committee wanted more emphasis on the direct value of renovations to students and the measures that would be taken to provide handicapped access. The direct value to students subsection took about half an hour to complete. For information on handicapped access, Alex realized that the architects needed to be consulted. A quick phone call later, Alex was told that the architect was in a meeting but would return the call within the hour. While waiting, Alex made the other changes, which, although trivial, took another half hour. It was 4:30 p.m. The architect called with the information. Alex added the new information and printed out a final copy at 4:45 p.m. A quick trip to the principal's office to make 15 copies, deliver the completed project to the district office (only five minutes away), and the job was done. However, the photocopier broke down half way through the copying at 4:52 p.m. Alex rushed the seven completed copies to the district office and arrived at 4:59 p.m. A request to make the extra copies and turn them in a few minutes late was granted by the superintendent, but with a warning that this was highly irregular and might jeopardize the grant. Alex was tired and frustrated but also elated to have completed the project.

Alex is a risk taker. Risk takers like excitement and adventure. Stress is both positive and negative to the risk taker. One problem risk takers have is in estimating their time appropriately; they generally underestimate the time it takes to complete any project. Presented below are activities and techniques Alex could have used to approach the problem in a different way.

Alex enjoys the pressure of meeting a deadline. Knowing that the task must be completed on time or everything will be lost keeps Alex's energy levels high. Alex also realizes that this intensity can inconvenience other people and result in feelings of frustration and anxiety. It was annoying to Alex to receive requests for changes on the grant proposal. On closer inspection Alex discovered that one of the reasons for the return was that a section had been left out of the proposal in the rush to meet the original deadline.

This time Alex had a month and decided to take a different approach, rather than rush to complete the proposal on the last day. The requests for changes were read carefully, and a To Do list was created. Interim time lines were prepared for completing such activities as contacting the architect and rewriting the justification section. Because the school photocopier was unreliable, Alex made arrangements to have the copies made in the district print shop three days before the final deadline. On a calendar in the library office Alex wrote the interim deadlines and checked on progress. If steps were appropriately completed, then Alex celebrated and relaxed. If activities were behind schedule, then Alex took time to readjust the schedule. The grant proposal was turned in two days early in a professional looking binding with page tabs. Alex received compliments from the superintendent on the timely receipt of the project and was told to expect the contractors Monday morning.

Case of the Vanishing Volunteers

Lee

It was two o'clock on a Thursday afternoon. Lee had just completed a satisfying project, recataloging all the books of criticism of American authors. The previous librarian had miscataloged the books both by call number and author number. Lee made call number changes and instead of author numbers used subject numbers. All books of criticism about Robert Frost were now together on the shelves. Lee felt the three weeks spent on this project were interesting and necessary.

Lee's next project was reorganizing the circulation desk and circulation system to make them more efficient. As Lee began the list of what was needed to complete the reorganization, a library volunteer interrupted with a serious question. "We have had three people quit in the past week. As of Friday there will only be enough volunteers to run the circulation desk 25 percent of the time. What shall we do?"

Lee was amazed. "We originally had 25 volunteers. How can three people who quit make such a difference?" Sandy, the volunteer coordinator, replied, "Ten volunteers have quit in the past two weeks. They are tired of working on recataloging books, refiling cards, and redoing spine labels. They wanted the job to involve work with the public as well as attending to details."

Lee, an organizer, was truly taken aback that everyone was not as interested in making certain that the small things were done correctly. Organizers enjoy working with details, lists, and charts. Organizers often have extensive To Do lists, clearly delineated schedules, and extensive working procedures. Although this attention to detail can smooth the running of an organization and improve decision making, organizers often fail to see the effect their methods have on others. They may be unaware of larger conceptual problems and spend time on interesting details rather than true priorities. Lee can use the following ideas to focus more clearly on the larger issues and the impact of an organizer's preferences.

The first response Lee had to the library volunteer's complaints about recataloging and redoing books was anger. "This job needed to be done. Who are they to complain? We are better off without them." After serious consideration, Lee decided perhaps it was too easy to become involved in the small and easily correctable problems and not deal with the larger issues. Obviously, one critical issue that had to be addressed was the volunteer's perception of their jobs. It would mean considerable time and staffing problems to the library if volunteers continued to quit at the current rate. Lee scheduled a meeting with both current and past volunteers and listened to their comments. Lee then asked for suggestions about steps for improving working conditions and feelings of satisfaction. Rather than making lists and creating procedures, Lee looked for broader issues and problems. In addition, Lee decided to carefully evaluate each new project for detail level and to balance details with broader conceptual plans.

Lee began to improve time management by acknowledging how uses of time and resources may conflict, trying to approach problems from a slightly broader perspective, and developing a clear understanding of priorities between detailed projects and longer term projects.

EFFECTIVE USE OF TIME

If some of the characteristics of all the librarians discussed above seem to fit you, you are not alone. Even though each person is unique, generalizations can be of help in understanding common time problems. Use any of the suggestions or techniques above that help you work with time. Do not limit yourself to the strategies suggested in any one category. As with all things, people may change over time. The strategies and techniques that work today may be modified in the future to deal with new problems and challenges. The important consideration is awareness of responses to time and identification of current challenges. No single way of using time is right or wrong. There are, however, ways to maximize the effectiveness of different preferences.

Case of Conflicting Styles

Conflicts in time use may also need to be resolved. Interacting with a supervisor, peer, student, volunteer, or family member whose time preferences are different from yours can lead to communication problems. If Chris (the information gatherer) was supervised by Dana (the achiever), Chris might receive poor performance evaluations. Dana might perceive Chris's lack of decision making as an inability to do the job appropriately. Chris, on the other hand, might see Dana's continuing striving for perfection as an obstacle to decision making. They could reinforce the negative components of each other's preferred time use methods.

It is important to identify the time conflicts that may result from different styles. Strategies for improvement in both personal time management and time management in relationships must be based on recognizing differences. The techniques that work for Dana may not be appropriate for Chris. One of Dana's responsibilities as a supervisor is to help Chris discover techniques and strategies that improve Chris's decision making without increasing anxiety. Chris's responsibility as an employee is to recognize Dana's time style differences. If Chris feels uncomfortable, then an assertive statement might be in order to open communication lines. Time use differences may or may not indicate job performance problems. It is important for each party in this relationship to differentiate between time use preferences and job performance.

Analysis procedures can be simply and easily used to identify your personal time challenges:

- Time out technique
- Simple time diary
- Reflective evaluation
- Activities checklist

BEGINNING TIME MANAGEMENT ANALYSIS PROCEDURES

Personality, situation, and level of commitment will affect the choice of techniques to begin time management. Presented below are simple techniques for analyzing time challenges. They focus attention on aspects of the environment that create time challenges. They are simply and quickly completed. Each analysis procedure may also be modified to increase the complexity of information gathered. As a beginning time manager, try out a technique that seems useful and practice it at a level that is comfortable. Later chapters will introduce more complex variations on these simple techniques.

Time out technique

A beginning strategy requiring little effort is to stop during the day and ask two questions: Is this the best possible use of my time? Would something else be more valuable or more useful? Asking these two simple questions will help you become aware of how you spend the day. Many times it is easier to engage in activities that result in minimum discomfort. These are like old shoes—they are always comfortable. However, they may not always be the most appropriate choice for the circumstances. The pressing need may be to develop a long-term technology plan. It may be easier to search for articles on the topic, create folders, and organize information than to start writing a plan. Disequilibrium from new or unfamiliar tasks can be disconcerting, even holding us back from beginning new projects. It is also an important time challenge.

Using the time out technique helps to identify tasks that are good uses of time. It also identifies tasks that may be less appropriate uses of time. Keep track of activities by jotting down what you are doing in two columns (see Figure 1). Keep the lists in a prominent place on your desk. When you ask yourself, "Is this the best possible use of my time?" and the answer is "Yes!" then write the activity down in one column. If the answer is "No!" then write the activity down in another column. Keep these records for a week.

To analyze, look at the lists and identify common elements in each column. Which tasks were good uses of time? Which tasks were less appropriate uses of time? The items in the good column might relate to helping students, teachers or library users, creating lesson plans or informational brochures and keeping up to date on new technology. The items in the less appropriate column might include routine clerical tasks and unneeded interruptions. The good column indicates that activities related to creating, implementing and reinforcing the service component of the librarian's job are important. These activities should be continued and time allocated to them increased. The tasks in the less appropriate column indicate activities that should be revised, eliminated, or delegated to someone else. Implementation techniques described in the section below and throughout the book may be used to revise, eliminate, or delegate activities identified through this analysis procedure.

Simple time diary

Another approach to examining time is keeping a time diary. The simple time diary does not require detailed entries throughout the day, as do complex time logs. To keep a simple time diary, set aside approximately five to ten minutes at the end of each day for a week or two. Briefly describe or list what you did. Do not try to censor or organize your recollections. Write down what you remember doing and who you interacted with during the day. It is not necessary to be exhaustive. This is a beginning activity to create awareness and to start understanding how time is used. Motivation will remain high if the diary does not become an overwhelming task. As a beginner at time management, take small steps and focus on completing what you begin (see Figure 2).

After a week, review what you have written. The process of writing will have identified some patterns already. Now begin a simple analysis and identify major categories of activities or people that account for your time use. For the second week use the diary to write about tasks which are time problems or challenges. By focusing on these areas, relationships between certain activities and time use will become more apparent.

Every time you pick up mail, is it an hour before you return to the library office? Until keeping the simple time diary, you might not have realized that chatting with a co-worker, stopping to look at the new flower beds, and reading your mail

FIGURE 1 Time out technique sample activity list

Example of an Activity List for a school library media specialist to answer the question: Is this actitivity the best possible use of my time?

YES	NO
• Creating a new info. skills lesson on search strategies using the online public access system.	• Reshelving materials students left after a lesson on habitats.
• Meeting with the science teacher to develop a new unit on endangered species.	• Replacing a burned out bulb in the math teacher's overhead. • Sorting mail.
• Helping a student understand why two books have different information about the causes of the Civil War.	• Cleaning tables with grafitti written on them.
• Training student assistants to check out/check in materials on the new circulation system.	• Looking for budget figures from two years ago to find out how much the VCR cost.

were completed before returning to the library office. This break may actually be an important use of time. It may represent a period when you refresh, revitalize, and prepare for the next segment of the day. On the other hand, it may be an expenditure of time that you did not recognize and wish to change. The time diary will help identify some of these areas and make your use of time more conscious and purposive. Your behavior may or may not change. However, the way you use your time will become more apparent.

Reflective evaluation

The reflective evaluation may be used by librarians who do not like to take notes or write down activities. A reflective evaluation may be completed with no written evidence. A

FIGURE 1 Cont.

Example of an Activity List for a public librarian to answer the question: Is this actitivity the best possible use of my time?

YES	NO
• Reading an article on new CD-ROM products.	• Listening to a salesperson describing their whole new product line.
• Designing a brochure for visually impaired library users that will be printed in large type.	• Fixing a broken lock on a file cabinet.
• Helping a regular library user find a new mystery book.	• Waiting for a late volunteer to arrive and take over the circulation desk.
• Introducing a new library user to the collection and check out procedures.	• Filing old supply catalogs.

reflective evaluation may also be written, recorded, or video taped. The object of a reflective evaluation is to examine activities that take significant amounts of time. The procedure focuses on thinking about those activities which consume a large portion of a librarian's day.

On the first day, create a mental or written list of the five activities that use the most time. Create broad categories and then estimate how much of a typical day each activity takes. Looking at things in larger segments than minutes and hours gives an impression of overall emphasis (see Figure 3).

From the five categories choose one activity that causes many time-related problems. The time problems may affect you, library staff, students, community members, or a combination of people. Think about the activity. What are the advantages of engaging in this activity? What are the disadvantages? Who is affected by the problems related to this activity?

At a first sitting, consider the categories, make time estimates, and begin thinking about the problem. Do this in 15 or

Figure 2 Simple time diary sample week

Monday, April 4

- Difficult day --assistants were absent due to flu--spent three hours at circ. desk.
- Continued making new shelf labels for stacks--teachers are complaining they can't find anything--students don't seem to have noticed any difference.
- VCR disappeared again--check J.Smith's room first and found it being used.
- Still looking for information on the Life Cycle Library series that P. Cooper wants. not in BIP. Check ILL?

Tuesday, April 5

- Cleaned out equipment room 5th and 6th period--very dusty--am still sneezing.
- 1st period found info. on Donner Party for student in A. Jones class.
- 2nd period--went to J. Smith's class and spoke on current scifi/fantasy authors.
- After school B. Piper was looking for e.e. cummings: the Art of His Poetry--ordered from the State Library.
- Went to pick up mail at 10:30am--didn't get back until noon--Sue in principal's office had questions about new book--read interesting new catalog and mail in faculty lounge.

Wednesday, April 6

- Had to fix TV#2 for J. Smith--Norm/Serv switch was in wrong position--while there spoke with Smith's Dept. chair about problems with scheduling and using VCRs. We will get together to talk about problems later.
- Group of student in to do research who were trouble--finally ended up placing at separate tables--Maybe tonight's Spring Dance is making them more excitable--usually a good class.

Thursday, April 7

- To tired to write--overwhelming day--2 classes per period all day.

Friday, April 8

- J. Smith's class in for early bird period--choosing Scifi/fantasy books.
- Student assistants finished four major projects: Biographies, Magazines lists, Shelf labels and VF list.
- General straightening and cleaning all day--Next week is SPRING BREAK!

FIGURE 3 Reflective list example

List of reflective categories for a librarian in a small one person public library

CATEGORY	% of day
Helping library users	50
Clerical (filing, sorting, shelving, etc.)	25
Circulation tasks	20
Management (budget, ordering, etc.)	3
Planning	2

20 minutes. A day or two later, set aside another 15 or 20 minutes to review your thoughts. This may be a mental or written list. Has anything new occurred to you? In the meantime, observe the problem more closely and add details to your original thoughts. Have you had any ideas that might help to change either the problem situation or your response to the problem? Think about these issues. Consider changes which might be made.

A day or two later, set aside 20 minutes. Collect your thoughts on what might improve the situation. Choose one option and carefully think through the consequences of implementing a change. Visualize how a library user might react, how a supervisor might react and how faculty members or library staff might react. Imagine yourself saying and doing things differently. Consider how you would feel. Think about which behaviors would be most effective. Perhaps an assertiveness technique would be appropriate. Picture the difference this change might make. If the positive outcomes outweigh possible discomfort then decide to change. Reflect on the situation one more time, practicing behaviors and anticipating responses in your mind. Set a specific date and time to begin the activity before you complete the session.

Activities checklist

An activities checklist is a quick method to obtain information on activities occurring frequently in the library. Checklists may be the outgrowth of another simple analysis procedure. For example, a simple time diary might result in a list of 15 common activities found in the library. A space at the end of the checklist can be created to write in additions. While this list would be the basis for an activities checklist, a checklist may be created using rational analysis only (see Figure 4).

Once the list is created, make a grid to indicate days or times. Put check marks by the appropriate activity, day, and time. This need not indicate how much time is spent in any one activity. It will identify which activities are engaged in most often. Tasks which are repeated often may be analyzed and procedures created to minimize their time commitment. Repetitive tasks are good candidates for time management techniques.

SIMPLE IMPLEMENTATION TECHNIQUES

In this section two beginning implementation techniques are described: creating To Do Lists and managing interruptions. While To Do lists may at first seem simple, there are actually many ways of creating and implementing To Do lists. A variation in technique might help revitalize your time management motivation. For librarians, interruptions are a major component of the job. This chapter covers simple approaches for getting the most out of interruptions and still feeling satisfied. Other common problems, such as managing paper and managing people, will be discussed in later chapters.

Creating To Do lists

To Do lists are the most common time management strategy. They are as simple as a list jotted on the back of an old envelope once a week and as complex as a database program that sorts and organizes activities by assigned priorities on an hourly basis. To Do lists are valuable when both function and form work for you. Essentially, a To Do list consists of the actions you wish to complete within a certain time frame. Your

Figure 4 Four examples of activities checklists

	AM	PM
Reference		
Circulation		
Acquistion		
Personal		
Clerical		
Other		

	M	Tu	W	Th	F	Sa
Administration						
Service						
Clerical						
Other						

	1	2	3	4	5	6
Consulting						
Teaching						
Reference						
Management						
Planning						
Clerical						
Other						

	Before School	AM	Lunch	PM	After School
Teacher questions					
Student questions					
Preparing lessons					
Delivering lessons					
Equipment					
Other					

TIME MANAGEMENT EXERCISE 5

Implementing a Simple Analysis Procedure

15-20 minutes per day for one week

1. Choose one of the analysis procedures described above.
2. Implement it for one week.
3. Analyze the results and create a short term plan to change two behaviors based on your analysis.
4. Keep track of the results and reward yourself (A new time management tape would be a good idea).

preferences and needs establish both the actions and the time frame. To create a To Do list format that works, consider the two main variables: actions to complete and time required. A third component, which combines the two variables together, is establishing priorities, and this will be discussed later.

Where do things to do come from? They come from user requests, telephone calls, mail, projects, classes, user suggestions, principals' demands, library board requests, articles read, policy decisions, technical problems, and committee meetings. There is a never ending supply of things to do. The first step in creating a To Do format is to decide how you want to record your list of things to do from all these sources. Some possible list format options are:

- On the back of envelopes and small pieces of paper as you think of ideas or as people make requests.
- On a desk calendar.
- In a notebook or diary.
- In a computer data base or word processor.
- On a yellow pad or tablet.
- In an appointment book.
- On a white board or chalk board.
- On printed To Do lists purchase from office suppliers.
- On a cassette tape.
- On activity forms such as those in *J.K. Lasser's Executives Personal Organizer Forms* (Goldstein 1988).
- Internally, on your own mental To Do list.

You may even decide to use a combination of these formats. For example, you might take notes on the back of envelopes and then transfer them to a yellow pad once a day. If you create and keep a To Do list, it is important to choose a method that is easy and convenient for you to maintain. The only good technique is the one that works for you.

The other major variable in creating To Do lists is the time period the list will cover. To Do lists may be created hourly, daily, weekly, monthly, yearly, or any combination thereof. The predominant type of To Do list is a daily schedule. This is usually a mixture of scheduled events such as committee meetings, job responsibilities, and personal appointments with activities the librarian also wishes to accomplish on the same day. This daily To Do schedule may be created from a master list of things the librarian wants to complete. Another common variation on To Do lists are weekly schedules and/or activities. Many librarians do not create a master To Do list in written form, but rather keep the list in their heads. In all formats, activities completed during any particular day or week are those that take priority due to either personal preference or outside pressure. Activities not completed during allotted time periods may or may not be moved to the next day or week.

The final, and probably most critical, element in creating To Do lists is the decision making or priority setting process that accompanies the format and time frame. Traditional time management approaches advocate two methods: sorting activities into prioritized categories or creating a prioritized list for a day, week, or month. In the sorting approach, activities are judged on the basis of how important each activity is. The activities are then placed in folders, notebook lists, or trays organized by priority. They are generally labeled as A, B, and C priorities or 1, 2, and 3 priorities. Only when all the A or 1 priorities have been completed will the next level be addressed. If the A level priorities are never completed, then the B level priorities are never attempted. This approach allows the librarian to identify the most important activities and to work on them until completed. On the other hand, something originally identified as a B or C activity may become an A activity because timely action has not been taken on it.

The other traditional approach to prioritizing a To Do list is to create a list of things to do today, or this week or this month. The underlying assumption is that the items chosen for today's To Do list are those that are most important to do today. Choices in this method may be based on outside deadlines, personal needs, and already scheduled events. The sorting process in this method is generally internal rather than external.

A less traditional approach, but one that is gaining popularity, is to sort activities by type. Reference items and questions to be answered are kept in one To Do list; faculty, supervisor, or community requests for services go in another. Administrative To Do activities are kept on another list. Technical or clerical activities are on another. Types of activities, rather than each different activity, are then prioritized. For example, all service requests and reference items would be completed before clerical activities were attempted (see Figure 5).

Variation of this approach focuses To Do priorities on different categories by time of day or by day of the week. For example, Monday mornings might be scheduled to complete To Do items related to administrative responsibilities, Tuesday afternoons for clerical and maintenance tasks, Wednesday midday for returning non-urgent phone calls. The advantage of this method is that like activities are grouped together and continuity may be maintained. The disadvantage is that a specific type of activity may not be able to wait until its assigned day or time. This method of sorting and prioritizing by type may help librarians make more appropriate choices about where and how to spend their time (see Figure 6).

Managing interruptions

One way to manage interruptions is to avoid them. A series of interruptions can have a strong negative impact on the successful completion of a project. The first interruption will slow momentum slightly, but soon you will be back on track. The second interruption requires more backtracking in order to return to the point at which you were interrupted. After the third or fourth interruption you may conclude that the job is impossible to complete today and go on to another activity. If this happens too often on the same project, you may begin to blame the project and not the interruptions. If the project becomes more and more difficult in your mind, it may never be completed.

Avoiding interruptions can be accomplished through communicating the need for time alone. One elementary school librarian posts a large and visible weekly schedule: 9 a.m. to 10 a.m. each day of the week is set aside for one library managerial task. Monday is cataloging, Tuesday is selection

FIGURE 5 Categorical To Do list format

Categorical format for use by school library media specialists.

Management	Student	Teacher	Clerical
1.			
2.			
3.			
4.			
5.			
6.			
7.			
8.			
9.			

Categorical format for use by public librarians.

Administration	Service	Reference	Clerical	Planning
1.				
2.				
3.				
4.				
5.				
6.				
7.				
8.				
9.				

and ordering, Wednesday is production, Thursday is collection evaluation, and Friday is planning. Of course, this is not the only time that these activities occur, but the librarian mini-

FIGURE 6 To Do by days of the week

	M	Tu	W	Th	F
AM	Long range planning		Phone calls	Reading	

	M	Tu	W	Th	F
PM		Clerical			Corres-pon-dence

mizes interruptions by indicating that administrative tasks have priority. Only emergency problems are handled during this time. Faculty, staff, and students have learned to ask questions or make requests before or after this time period. When emergencies do arise or exceptions need to be made, the librarian is pleasant and willing to comply.

Because service responsibilities are the primary factor in the one-person library, developing uninterrupted time may be more complex. Recommendations for decreasing interruptions in the one-person library include: scheduling one to two hours of work time a week when the library is not open, finding volunteer help from seniors, students, or community organizations, and identifying quiet times and planning their use.

Telephone interruptions can be most annoying. In public and academic libraries, telephone calls are part of the reference process and must be answered whether convenient or not. Telephone calls in school libraries are different. Few phone calls to school libraries require answering reference questions or requests. Although most calls are personal, procedural, or financial, they may have as strong a demand-based need as those for public or academic libraries.

It is possible to avoid telephone interruptions in all types of libraries, but the advantages and disadvantages must be carefully weighed. Unplugging phones, using answering machines, or refusing to answer the phone are viable options, particularly when an activity requires intense concentration and must be completed within a certain time frame. Used wisely and only when necessary, the shut down of telephone interruptions can be an effective time management method. Certainly, the possibilities of emergency needs should be carefully considered and alternative notification options created.

If avoiding telephone calls is not possible under normal library operating conditions, the interruptions caused by telephones may be minimized through applying the following techniques:

- Limit calls during working hours to five minutes.
- Assertively say no to sales people you do not wish to speak with.
- Establish as quickly as possible what the caller needs or wants.
- Take appropriate notes on who called, the caller's phone number, and what is to be done.
- Transfer calls that others can or should be answering.
- Return the call when more convenient.
- Indicate to switchboard or secretarial staff when phone calls will interrupt critical activities.
- Establish policies and procedures for the use of the phone by others.

The most effective method for minimizing interruptions is to state assertively what your needs and expectations are regarding the interruption. You have the right to minimize interruptions as long as you also take into account others' needs and your service responsibility. Consistency in behavior is a critical factor in reducing the number of interruptions. Inconsistent behavior such as saying, "I am busy now, but I can speak to you for five minutes," and then carrying on a conversation for 20 or 30 minutes indicates that you really were not busy. The next time, the caller will expect you to talk

TIME MANAGEMENT EXERCISE 6

Using an Implementation Technique

15-20 minutes a day for one week

This exercise works well when started at the beginning of a five day week. However, it can be started at any time. It helps to compare and make choices between different time management techniques. One often expressed problem with time management is that people discover even a new activity to be boring after a short time period. This exercise is a way of minimizing boredom and helping choose a technique that demonstrates positive results.

1. When reading through the suggestions of implementation techniques, choose one or two which appeal to you.
2. You may also choose a technique you have heard about or read about that you would like to try.
3. Write the techniques down in your notebook or on your calendar.
4. From among the techniques you have chosen, identify one to begin in the morning.
5. Try the technique for two days.
6. Choose a second technique and try it for two days.
7. At the end of the fourth day, make a decision. Which technique worked best? Had the most positive results? Drop the other technique.
8. Continue implementing the chosen activity for another day. Make a final decision. Is this worth my time and effort to continue? Does it make a significant difference?
9. Whatever your decision, you will have learned a valuable lesson about time management and your personal preferences. Reward yourself with a walk in the park or a drive in the country.

at length no matter what you say. If you make a statement about the length of time you are available, then keep to your request. Consistently matching words to actions will result in people accepting the limitations you establish and reduce interruptions.

PLANNING FOR SUCCESSFUL TIME MANAGEMENT

The librarian just beginning time management should consider simple planning activities. Complex strategies may be integrated later. At this stage, it is important to focus on small steps that result in immediate success. The To Do list discussed above is an example of a simple planning strategy. It involves sorting, prioritizing, and scheduling activities for today and for the future. The first part of this section contains a conceptual discussion that defines planning as an approach to "doing the important things." The second part examines three simple planning strategies for short-, medium-, and long-term time management.

DOING THE IMPORTANT THINGS

Beginning time managers need to focus on doing the important things. Important things are identified through planning: short term, medium term, and long term. Questions to consider in identifying the important things include: What are your life goals? What are your work goals? What is important to you? What is important to keep you employed? Are these things compatible? If they are not, what are you going to do? What are you willing to do? What are the expectations for excellence in your organization? What are the expectations for competent performance? Will you be able to keep your job if you are competent but not necessarily excellent in all things? What area of excellence would most satisfy you?

Answers to these question will help identify the important things—things that are important to you and things that are important for your job. If there is a gap between what you consider to be important and your job requirements, a serious assessment may be necessary. Perhaps you can make changes to match your job requirements more closely to your values and beliefs. Do what you can within the limits of what is possible, but also try to stretch the limits, changing them to meet your needs and expectations.

If your idea of what is important conflicts significantly with those around you, you may need let people know what you are doing and why. State your goals and objectives explicitly and repeatedly. Convince people that your choices fit within a strategy to achieve these goals and objectives. Objectives statements can not be made often enough nor can they be said too plainly. People who know your goals and objectives will be less likely to believe that your decisions are arbitrary and less likely to ask for things you are unwilling to do. You will be able to say *no* more reasonably and to have your decisions accepted. Communicating clearly is a critical element in creating time to do the important things.

Know why you are doing what you are doing. Start to develop an internal alarm clock that goes off when time is passing and you are not doing important things. For example, when you are angry it might be difficult to think. Anger may cause you to spend hours on something of minimal importance. If you are angry, it may be important to deal with the anger rather than sublimate it in trivial details. It may be more satisfying to deal directly with the person or problem. If that is not possible, working off the physical effects of anger by going for a walk or deep breathing can help maintain focus. It is more important to relax than to engage in a flurry of unimportant activity. Work completed when angry may need to be repeated because it was done haphazardly. It also could create more work than was necessary but, once started, had to be finished.

Case of Furniture Frustration

Casey was the librarian in a midsize rural community. Once, in a fit of pique over a group of teenagers who were causing problems in the library, Casey decided to rearrange the furniture. The original arrangement created blind spots where teenagers could not be seen easily. The new arrangement turned out to be effective but took two weeks to complete. At the end of the first week, Casey was tired of the project and was beginning to think about the time spent.

A more reasonable course of action would have been to deal directly with the teenagers who were causing problems. Then Casey, who ended up moving most of the furniture personally, could have implemented the rearrangement over a longer time and with custodial help. At the time, moving furniture was a way for Casey to work off frustration with physical work. However, the frustration dissipated after the first half day. By that time, the furniture was so out of order that it took the rest of the week to straighten it out and another week to create the appropriate environment. Casey's internal alarm should have started ringing almost immediately. A short walk or some deep breathing exercises would have served the same purpose as moving furniture.

Doing the important things requires planning what you

want to do—and what you do not want to do. It is sometimes necessary to refuse or put aside some projects, or complete them cursorily in order to have the time and energy to do the important things. This can create frustration. When you are doing important things, the satisfaction should outweigh the guilt and frustration of not doing other things. Doing the important things may initially create discomfort because important things can be difficult and time-consuming. It is necessary to develop a balance among different types of important activities.

Assertive behavior can be an essential strategy in doing the important things. As a responsible professional, you make choices and set goals that reflect the philosophy and needs of the library and the users. You also maintain standards and values, which must be woven into how you choose to perform important activities. The stronger your personal commitment to the value of the activities that you have chosen, the easier it will be for you to be assertive about your rights, the rights of coworkers, and the rights of library users to benefit from your professional expertise. Being assertive does not mean being pushy or aggressive any more than it means being passive. It means that you have a right to do the things that are important to you.

Choose a strategy and start to plan:

- Short term
- Medium term
- Long term

THREE PLANNING STRATEGIES

Doing the important things includes short-term, medium-term, and long-term commitments. Immediate accomplishments will keep daily motivation high. Tasks to be finished in the near future can focus on more depth and substance to maintain motivation. Long-term projects may change lives and make the organization a better place. This array of activities will provide greater satisfaction if a short-term activity does not work out. It also helps you to make difficult choices when a new problem is added to your list. You will be able to decide if the immediate problem is worth destroying the chances for completion of the long-term project. For example, is speaking with three salespeople as important as developing a plan for patrons with learning disabilities to use library facilities more effectively? In order to do the important things, you will choose not to do the less important things.

Short-term planning includes day-to-day and weekly activities. To Do lists, calendars, and daily diaries are the most prominent implementation techniques for short-term planning. Often librarians refer to short-term planning as

TIME MANAGEMENT EXERCISE 7

Beginning Planning—15 minutes

The purpose of this exercise is to create a simple plan for maintaining your commitment to time management.

1. Find a large sheet of paper, preferably large enough to hang on a wall and be seen from a distance.
2. Using felt markers in three different colors, draw three large circles on the paper.
3. Label one circle work, one circle personal and one circle home/family.
4. In each circle, write one reason why improving time management would be beneficial to this aspect of your life. For example, in the personal circle you might write, “I like reading science fiction novels and would like to read more.” In the home/family circle you might write, “I want to be more relaxed and comfortable at home.”
5. You may write more than one reason if you wish, but one reason should be sufficient to begin. This is a beginning exercise. Reasons do not have to be the most important thing you can think of. This is practice.
6. When you get discouraged or find a technique or procedure is not working, look at your circles and reasons.
7. Focus on why you wanted to make changes. If the reasons are not longer valid, choose new ones.
8. It is easy to lose motivation, if positive new outcomes are not kept clearly in mind. Use this chart as a plan for keeping motivated and moving in the direction of improved time management.

scheduling. Tasks and activities to be completed are scheduled into the day. Short-term planning can easily become a reactive activity: as a problem or issue arises, it is scheduled into the day or the week. The relative importance of the task may not be evaluated in terms of medium-term or long-term priorities. Focusing on day-to-day activities can mean that medium- or long-range projects are never completed. It is essential to balance short-term planning and use of time with appropriate time use for activities that will take longer blocks of time.

Keeping up with everyday problems can become an unending cycle of crisis management. Previously discussed time management techniques can partially alleviate daily interruptions and crises. When immediate time constraints become overwhelming, a different approach may be required. Spencer Johnson's *One Minute for Myself* (1985) can be used to develop new ways to integrate activities. The technique helps you regain perspective when you are faced with the unending demands of the short term.

Medium-term planning involves looking at monthly or quarterly activities and priorities. Common implementation techniques related to medium-term planning are objectives, calendars, and project charts. Medium-term planning may be forgotten in the rush to complete day-to-day activities and the excitement of long-range activities. Medium-term planning has strong evaluative components. Implementation for medium-term planning can include checkpoints along the way to see that short-term activities are not overwhelming your use of time. It can also help you to judge how things are coming for long-term projects. In addition, medium-term planning can help keep motivation high by reinforcing the good things you are doing and helping to eliminate activities that consume time but that do not have positive results.

In midyear it may be important to reevaluate long-term goals. Intervening activities, time commitments, and crises may have changed your direction. Quarterly goals, such as those suggested by McCay (1959), can bring long-term priorities back into focus. McCay's quarterly objectives cover both personal and work components. They help reevaluate long-term perspectives and provide needed short-term motivation.

Long-term planning encompasses a year or longer. Strategic planning and goal statements are usually part of long-range planning activities and will be discussed in detail in Chapter Four. As a beginning time manager it is important for you to have a vision of where you want to go and what is important to you in your personal and professional life. At the beginning of a year, create long-term goals and identify long-range activities. This is the time to seriously consider the balance between work and personal life. *How to Get Control of Your Time and Your Life* (Lakein 1973) provides one approach for developing life goals that can help you determine the relative importance of personal and work goals and priorities.

Your personal approach to time management will influence how you integrate the three different levels of planning. A multitasker may be most comfortable moving from level to level, never focusing on any one way of making time decisions. For multitaskers, integrating time management in this random fashion could actually increase motivation. A conceptualizer may want to focus almost exclusively on the long term. It is, therefore, important for conceptualizers to integrate medium-term and immediate perspectives into a time integration plan. Time management should be a dynamic, reflective system rather than a static, completed system. It reflects work and personal priorities at all levels of planning.

CREATING A BEGINNING TIME MANAGEMENT SYSTEM

This chapter examined techniques for beginning and implementing time management activities in the library. No technique is suitable for all people; you will have your own preferences, styles, and needs. No technique is useful all of the time; your strategies, problems, and needs change with time and changing circumstances. This chapter provided a range of alternatives and choices to practice with, to use, and to discard if necessary. Some will work; some will not. Pick techniques that fit your natural ways. Then give the techniques time to work. Do not quit immediately. If the techniques do not work after a reasonable period of time, then try something new. This is a trial and error process. If a technique has been working well for a while and you find yourself dissatisfied or unhappy, return to this chapter and try something new. A new approach may provide a different perspective on your work. All the techniques here are useful. All can be successful. The choices and implementation must rest on your commitment to changing the way you think about time, plan your time, and respond to other people's demands on your time.

It is important not to be discouraged if one strategy or procedure does not work. Instead, analyze the problems you found with the technique:

- Was the problem created because the strategy or procedure was inherently counter to your own personality or way of doing things?
- Did a problem occur because a strategy or procedure conflicted dramatically with the general manner in which your organization usually works?
- Was the strategy or procedure too difficult (time consuming) to continue on a regular basis?

- Was the strategy or procedure ineffective because it did not essentially change anything?
- Did the strategy or procedure seem too easy so you considered it less than worth while?
- If you stopped using a strategy or procedure, why did you stop?
- Did you really try to make the strategy or procedure work? What might have interfered with your motivation to implement the strategy or procedure?

Time management is a case of successive approximations. The more you work to understand what works for you and why, the better your time management will become. Do not become complacent. Always have alternatives, even on a temporary basis, if one technique ceases to work or becomes boring.

The task before you is to choose from the strategies and techniques suggested in the chapter and to create a simple time management system. The system will be in the form of an action plan. The plan itself should take no longer than ten or 15 minutes to create, and it should require no more than ten or 15 minutes each day to implement. You will need to integrate the time management strategies and techniques discussed in this chapter into a systematic plan. This plan should be developed to result in success and lead you to more advanced activities. Once the plan is created, you may wish to practice for one or two weeks before reading more. You may also wish to read ahead to Chapter Three and examine other options.

Your time management system will consist of the five components discussed earlier: motivation, self awareness, analysis procedures, implementation techniques, and planning strategies. For each of these components you will choose a simple action step to be accomplished within the next week or two. Librarians who prefer recipes may follow the approach outlined below. In this system, decisions are made within narrow limits and choices are prescribed. It is a useful approach for librarians who want to begin with the minimum amount of decision making. A more flexible plan follows which allows librarians to create their own time management system. This second plan provides a framework but leaves the decisions about how, when, and what up to the individual librarian. It is designed for the librarian who wants to create a system tailored specifically to personal needs and goals.

RECIPE FOR BEGINNING TIME MANAGEMENT

Day 1: Create a motivation chart as described in Exercise 7 with specific outcomes. Refer to this often during the two weeks to reinforce and keep your motivation high.

Day 2: Choose the time use approach which most closely matches your characteristics. Choose only one for this initial recipe. Keep these time use preferences in mind as you make the choices discussed below.

Day 2: Choose the analysis procedure which best matches your time use preference and apply it for one week (Days 2 through 6).

Day 6: Summarize the findings from your analysis procedure. Reflect on the things you discovered that surprised or interested you.

Day 7: Choose an implementation technique to match your time use preference and that will impact one of your findings from Day 6.

Day 7: Implement the technique (Days 7-10) and keep mental or written notes on how you felt, what worked and what did not.

Day 10: Reflect on the technique and reward yourself for trying.

Day 10: Create a simple plan for what you wish to do next with time management.

Choose from one of the following simple plans or make one of your own.

- Read Chapter 2 again and choose different time management exercises.
- Read Chapter 3 and start advancing time management.
- Buy a motivational time management tape and follow the directions (Bliss 1986; Blanchard 1990; Branden 1990; Elgin 1990; LeBoeuf 1987; Mackenzie 1984, 1988; Winston 1989).
- Create your own approach to time management.

- Take a break and try this again in a week, a month, or a year.

The important aspect of this planning recipe is that you consciously choose what you wish to do next. If time management has ceased to be important, then drop it. Let it be a reasoned choice. You will feel more confident, successful, and happy if you have chosen your next steps carefully.

FLEXIBLE SYSTEM FOR BEGINNING TIME MANAGEMENT

This section suggests a process for creating a time management system but does not prescribe the elements, the time frame, or the range of activities. This is a way for you to create your own plan, within your own needs and requirements. It asks that you consider the five components of a time management system but does not require that you utilize them. Follow the steps below to create your own time management system:

1. Establish a trial time period to practice time management. A minimum of one week or a maximum of three would be appropriate for beginning time management. The choice is yours. Pick the time frame and fit information from the following into your preferred time limits.
2. Consider the five components of a time management system: motivation, self-awareness, analysis procedures, implementation techniques, and planning strategies. Decide which of these you are most interested in implementing. You may choose one, none, or all. Make a mental or written list of those you will work on.
3. Choose activities, strategies, procedures, or exercises to try out during the time frame you have established. You may develop a schedule about when and where you will do these activities. Alternatively, you may randomly choose to try out different exercises or processes as they strike your fancy.
4. Keep a mental or written record of your feelings, responses, and successes.
5. At the end of the time frame chosen, reflect on the usefulness of the activities, the way they were implemented, and your responses.
6. Create a plan for how you wish to proceed next. You

may choose to repeat this process. You may go on to Chapter Three for advanced time management information. You may choose to focus on one of the beginning planning ideas suggested in this chapter. You may choose another book, tape, or process entirely. If time management is still important to you, make a simple-to-follow plan the next stage in your time management system.

Case of the Befuddled Beginner

Beginning time management system example

After reading about time management, Tracy decided to create a simple and easy-to-follow plan for improving time management. After looking at the recipe and the more open approach, she chose to create a flexible plan. Tracy's time frame was to be one week. This seemed about as far in advance as she could consider, and she believed that her motivation would remain high for one week. Choosing the time frame was as much time as Tracy wanted to spend considering motivation, so no activities were chosen during the week to increase motivation. While reading through the time use preferences, Tracy felt strongly that the conceptualizer method was most familiar, but decided it was not important to work with this preference.

Tracy viewed analysis procedures as a logical activity and randomly picked the simple time diary. At the end of each day Tracy wrote down what she remembered about the day's activities. On Wednesday, Tracy realized this was more difficult than expected. After a tiring day, she found it difficult to remember everything that had happened and those things she did remember were uncomfortable to write about since she had felt angry and frustrated for most of the day. Tracy wrote down a few sentences anyway: "Had a bad day. Nothing went right. Didn't seem to have time to do anything," and left it at that. The next day was quiet, and at the end of the day Tracy wrote her commentary on the day but also a few more insights into the day before. Time had softened some of the difficulties. On Friday, Tracy was tired but happy to have completed an analysis each day.

Reflecting on the activity, Tracy realized that the busier it was, the harder it was to remember everything she had done. It seemed apparent that the days when it would be most valuable to have information were the days it was most difficult to get information. She created a simple plan for the next week. Tracy knew that Wednesday was going to be a busy day again and that it would be impossible to keep track of what was going on, but that it would be interesting to know. Tracy had a full-time assistant, who could keep notes on Tracy's day. It was an unusual request, but Tracy was concerned about what happened during those very busy times. Tracy would keep the simple diary for each day except Wednesday. On Wednesday, Tracy would get notes from the assistant on what had occurred.

In addition, Tracy decided that motivation was actually more difficult to keep up than anticipated. The purchase of a *One Minute Manager* (Blanchard 1990) audiotape was a reward for completing the week and for improving motivation for the next week.

Tracy's story is a simplified example of a time management system that demonstrates basic pitfalls. It is easy to fall into patterns of behavior because they are familiar. For example, Tracy's failing to acknowledge the problems of conceptualizers was typical of that approach. Not writing down much on Wednesday was also a conceptualizer problem. Conceptualizers have difficulty keeping detailed notes such as those required for a daily diary. Tracy's decision to be observed on the next Wednesday was an excellent choice for a conceptualizer. Outside reporting will make it easier for Tracy to see and accept routine and continuous activities.

3 EXTENDING THE COMMITMENT

Extending the commitment to time management focuses on advanced knowledge of the five components of a time system:

Motivating to do
Understanding space use
Creating detailed analyses
Managing paper
Putting out fires

The previous chapter explored making a commitment to time management. This chapter examines extending that commitment to time management through advanced procedures and techniques. Chapter Two focused on changing actions and creating more effective time use. This chapter emphasizes the difference between knowing and doing. Knowing indicates that information has been acquired, but doing implies putting the knowledge into practice. It is possible to have detailed knowledge about time management but have difficulty in implementing the knowledge. Successfully translating from knowing to doing is discussed as a motivational component of time management. Awareness of one's environment is explored through examining how librarian's organize space. More detailed processes for examining librarian's time challenges are described in the analysis procedures section. There are also specific implementation techniques for managing paper. Finally, planning is addressed in dealing with crises. Differences between crises, interruptions, and time management are explored As in the previous chapter, time management exercises and examples are provided as guides. At the end of the chapter there is a process for integrating knowledge into a more advanced time management system for doing.

THE DIFFERENCE BETWEEN KNOWING AND DOING

The transition between knowing and doing is difficult. We may know how to do something, but problems arise in the implementation. Knowledge of how to plan, to organize time, to maximize time usage, the pitfalls of time management, and many different ways of focusing on time may be clear. This knowledge does not necessarily make doing easier. There may be obstacles. Earlier patterns of behavior may interfere with implementation. Expectations of success or failure will also affect choices of doing or not doing. Knowledge may appear to be value free, but emotions, feelings, and values are attached to activities and actions. It may be easier to return to old patterns of behavior than to continue applying the new knowledge.

What can be done to ease the transition from knowing to doing? Choose activities resulting in professional success or personal satisfaction. This makes doing seem more pleasant and rewarding. While for some people the transition from knowing to doing is completed through plans, goals, and actions steps for others the transition is more random. One choice might be to implement a new strategy for one week. Another option is to develop a different perspective on the problem. A third strategy is to add complementary techniques to existing time management activities. Knowing about motivation, self-awareness, analysis procedures, implementation techniques, and planning strategies translates into the following implementation activities:

Use these activities to move from knowing about time management to doing something specific.

Knowing about motivation for time management could be translated into these activities:

- Reading books, listening to audiotapes, or watching videotapes
- Creating discussion groups to reinforce time management commitment
- Working through a single book and applying the ideas
- Choosing a time management philosophy that matches time preferences
- Practicing proactive behaviors

Knowing about self-awareness could be translated into these activities:

- Identifying personal time preferences or space use preferences
- Practicing self-esteem activities
- Practicing assertiveness activities
- Choosing techniques that are comfortable to implement
- Identifying conflicts in time or space use preferences with colleagues

TIME MANAGEMENT EXERCISE 8

Translating from Knowing to Doing—10 minutes

1. Take 3 minutes and write down as many techniques, strategies and ideas as you can think of for managing time. Just keep writing until you run out of time.
2. Take 1 minute and add to or revise the list if you wish.
3. Circle the time management activities you currently use.
4. Choose one *new* activity to do this week and do it for the whole week. Evaluate its effectiveness.
5. Reward yourself for the new activity and the activities you already do. (Buy a new desk organizer, notebook or pen to use when you work on time management projects.)

Knowing about time analysis procedures could be translated into these activities:

- Filling out a chart or time diary twice a day
- Writing a journal of impressions and feelings for ten minutes each day for a week
- Tallying activities on a checklist sheet regularly for two or three weeks
- Asking a secretary or clerical assistant to take notes on time use
- Taking a random sample of activities using a timer or watch
- Videotaping or audiotaping portions of the day

Knowing about implementation techniques could be translated into these activities:

- Working on a specific problem such as paper management for two weeks
- Creating and applying a new type of To Do list
- Minimizing interruptions by setting a timer on phone calls
- Closing the office door each day for one half hour of thinking time

- Doing something not quite perfectly and not feeling guilty
- Purchasing a new desk organizer, calendar or diary

Knowing about planning strategies could be translated into these activities:

- Writing three goals to be worked on in the next four months
- Developing one personal, one work and one family-related priority
- Posting library objectives prominently in your office and in the library
- Creating one long-term activity to discuss at the next staff meeting.

HOW LIBRARIANS ORGANIZE SPACE

In the previous chapter six ways of using time were examined. This section looks at six methods for organizing space that are clustered around three dimensions: location, arrangement, and function. Location is a measure of where things are placed within the available space. Arrangement examines how librarians distribute materials throughout space. Function indicates the way librarians choose to use space for maximum effect. The two ends of the location dimension are visible and invisible. The ends of the arrangement dimension are formal and casual. The ends of the function dimension are functional and creative. As with time use preferences, no way of organizing space is more right or more appropriate. These categories are simply ways of understanding how librarians manage their space and of identifying common patterns.

Understanding not only the way you use space but also the preferences of your coworkers or supervisors can minimize conflicts and increase communication. Librarians organize and use space in two very different environments. In an office or desk area a librarian is involved with personal space. The library facility itself is a public space. The styles of organization and arrangement in these two spaces may coincide with the librarian's personal style, or they may be different, based on demands from the librarian's organization. In this first section, personal space preferences are discussed and examples of the six space use preferences given. Following is a discussion of public space and of the differing needs that may affect how a librarian's personal space style is reflected in public space.

Librarians who prefer things visible or invisible are the opposite ends of the location dimension of space use. Visible space use includes librarians who want to be able to see and access materials openly at all times. These librarians want things to be immediately available. Those who prefer the visible find it too difficult and time-consuming to retrieve items from closets, drawers, and desks. On the other hand, a librarian who prefers the invisible believes that control comes from empty space. Materials that are out of sight indicate to this librarian that he or she is in full charge of the situation.

The second dimension of space use is arrangement. Arrangement is the method librarians use to organize materials irrespective of whether they are in sight or out of sight. The formal organizer may have materials in plain view or hidden, but in either case, all items are tidy and straight. The librarian equates neatness with organization. The casual organizer, on the other hand, gives the appearance of randomness. Things may be stacked on corners of desks, overflowing cabinets, or jumbled in drawers. Often the librarian with a casual space use preference saves everything because someday someone might just need that pamphlet, article, piece of string, or used box.

Function is the final space use dimension, representing both use of space and display of materials. The librarian who uses space with a functional approach is generally concerned with productivity and efficiency. The aesthetic aspects of the environment are secondary; things are organized for the best work effect. Creative space users, on the other hand, are too busy creating to be worried about organizational aspects of space. They focus on aesthetic considerations and projects.

Each of the ways of using and organizing space is a simplification and a characterization of extreme examples. However, they serve to demonstrate common problems that librarians must address when organizing space. After reading the descriptions below, try to identify the space use of the character presented. Take notes on or remember activities discussed for space use preferences that most closely match your own. Take notes or remember other techniques that seem interesting or useful.

Case of the Copped Copies

Jan

Jan rushed into the library office from a meeting with the Friends of the Library. A group was due in five minutes for an introduction to using the new online public access catalog (OPAC). A worksheet had been prepared for practice, and Jan needed to find the copies of the worksheet and the OPAC brochures. Since the worksheet copies should have been returned from the copier earlier in the day, Jan looked at the in-box first. The in-box, however, was overflowing with papers, catalogs, today's mail, and computer documentation. It was difficult to identify new items. Jan sorted through approximately half the box before deciding the copies were not there. Even though the rest of the desk was covered with three layers of paper, Jan knew what was in each layer. There was no evidence that anything had been moved or added. The papers were not disturbed.

In desperation, Jan pulled out the desk chair and sat down to think, then quickly jumped up. There were the worksheet copies with a note: "I knew you wouldn't be able to find these if I put them on your desk." Now Jan needed to find the brochures. The bookshelves behind the desks contained stacks of brochures for each library function. This made it easier to find the right subject instantly, without hunting through drawers and file cabinets. Jan went immediately to the appropriate stack and found the OPAC brochure.

Jan has a visible space use preference. As this brief description shows, having items in plain sight is not necessarily inefficient. It can, however, be disconcerting to those you work with. It also can mean that you spend time looking for items that are out but not necessarily available. Presented below are some techniques Jan could use to help improve the efficiency of the environment and still have things out and available.

After Jan attended a seminar on managing paper, it was apparent that something could be done to work with a preference for visible materials. The first step Jan took was to evaluate paper and other materials in the office. On a calendar, Jan made a personal appointment for today and for three months from today: "Review what is out. Put away things I am not using." Jan also purchased transparent stacking trays for the shelving behind the desk and large bulletin boards for the walls. The transparent trays helped Jan identify content more quickly. The bulletin boards increased the available space for keeping things visible. Jan decided to keep the in-box cleared daily and established a routine. First thing each morning, items were removed from the in-box, sorted, and placed in an appropriate stack on the desk, tacked on the bulletin board, or filed in the new stacking trays. One space, the in-box, always had the most current items without other layers obscuring the new information.

Case of the Bungled Budget

Lynn

When people walked into Lynn's office, they often said, "You need some posters on your wall. Did you just move in?" The walls of Lynn's office were bare. The desk had a single item on it: a combination calendar and desk pad. The shelves behind Lynn's desk contained books only. There were no papers, no stacks of mail to read, no unsightly piles of things to do. Lynn's phone was in a desk drawer, along with an answering machine and phone books.

It was 10:25 a.m., and Lynn was preparing to attend an 11:00 a.m. math department meeting. One of the items on the agenda was identifying equipment purchases for the next school year. Lynn was to bring pricing information, repair estimates, and longevity figures for video equipment. Opening the equipment catalog cabinet, Lynn realized that she had not filed the new catalogs. As they arrived in the mail, in order to keep office space tidy, Lynn had stacked them in the bottom drawer of the cabinet. After 15 minutes of sorting through catalogs, she found the appropriate items. She then put the rest of the catalogs back in the drawer for filing later.

For repair estimates Lynn called the district media services office. Underneath the telephone in the desk drawer were a stack of handwritten messages with telephone numbers on them. Lynn put them on the empty desk space and sorted through until the number for Shannon in media services surfaced. A ten-minute phone call later, Lynn had the basic information on repairs. She quickly moved the notes with phone numbers back into the drawer, on top of the telephone, to keep the desk top free. While Lynn was looking through the To Be Filed drawer for the article on longevity of video equipment, the telephone rang. She opened the drawer and picked up the receiver. Slips with phone numbers scattered over the floor and under the desk. The phone call was from the chair of the math department. "Did you forget our meeting, Lynn? It's 11:20, and we cannot do the budget without your figures."

Lynn prefers to have things invisible, but clear desk tops and empty spaces do not necessarily mean a person is in control or organized. Often people who put things out of sight have the same problems as people with materials in plain view. The problems are simply hidden in drawers and cabinets. Since control is important to people who prefer items to be out of sight, the strategies below provide the maximum degree of control. They also suggest ways for people with an invisible space preference to improve the efficiency of their space use.

After the problems with the math department budget meeting, Lynn was convinced it was important to improve filing. In order to keep external spaces clean, it was easiest to take a stack of catalogs and drop them in a drawer. It was too difficult and time-consuming to stand or crouch at the file cabinet to sort the catalogs. Lynn solved this problem by purchasing a rolling cart. As catalogs arrived in the mail, Lynn sorted them on the desk and immediately put them in the appropriate category in the rolling cabinet. The cabinet was rolled out of the office and made available to teachers and students. Another simple system that Lynn created to keep phone numbers together was an open filing box with broad category dividers.

When Lynn wrote down a new telephone number, she dropped the piece of paper behind the appropriate divider. The box was chosen to fit just behind the telephone in the desk drawer. Finally, Lynn bought new dividers for the To Be Filed drawer. Instead of stacking items together, she roughly sorted them by category and put them in the drawer. Articles and photocopies went in one divider. Bills, financial papers, and receipts in another divider. Requests for lessons, lessons plans, and instructional units went in another. It only took a few more minutes each day for Lynn to implement these simple systems, but these minutes saved time by improving the retrieval of information.

Case of the Fussy Filer

Jerry

In Jerry's office all the books were placed neatly on the shelves. Each shelf had exactly the same amount of books, and they were all even with the shelf edge. Jerry's desk had papers stacked in rows with no overlap. Pencils were precisely placed at a 90-degree angle to the desk edge. For Jerry, neatness equaled organization. One day Jerry decided to clean out and reorganize the office filing cabinets. The filing structure was too simple. Too many items were ending up in the same file folder. Fifteen hours later Jerry was just completing the reorganization and typing up new labels for the dividers in the file cabinets. It had been a long and difficult day, and Jerry would not finish for another two hours, until subject cards had been typed for each of the new file folders in the cabinets.

As with Jan and Lynn, Jerry's way of organizing papers and materials may not reflect the ability to use information. Jerry prefers a formal organizational structure. Formal organization, however, is not necessarily more appropriate or more useful than any other space use preference. The external space gives the impression of perfect organization, but the time required to keep up the formal structure may interfere with completing tasks. Librarians who prefer the formal approach can use the strategies discussed below to keep the neatness they appreciate but minimize the time consumed.

This was the fourth night in a week that Jerry arrived home late. Jerry's family felt neglected. They complained and said maybe it was time for Jerry to think about another job. While sitting alone with a cup of lukewarm coffee and a cold dinner, Jerry decided that maybe something could be done differently. Perhaps a complex job, such as reorganizing a filing system, did not need to be completed all at once. Jerry wrote a note to tack on the bulletin board in the library office: "Divide large jobs into small pieces. Do one small piece a day!" Jerry also decided to make a list of incentives to help remember to examine priorities and change systems that did not work. When a new step was taken that would result in a disruption of formal structure, Jerry purchased an appropriate organizing accessory. For example, when budget categories changed and the office system needed updating to match the new budget categories, Jerry was unhappy. The old files were tidy, well-prepared, and neatly typed. As an incentive to change the system, Jerry purchased folders and dividers for arranging the new budget categories in a color coded array.

Case of Ecological Necessity

Marty

Marty knew there was no better job in the world than being a librarian. It was your job to keep everything that everyone would ever need to answer any question anyone would ever ask. Marty had filled four filing cabinets in the library office and was currently looking at supply catalogs, trying to decide whether three or four more cabinets would be sufficient to store the materials that were stacked on the floor and under the desk. On top of the bookshelves in Marty's office were boxes stacked to the ceiling from book orders, equipment purchases, and supply orders. Falling out of one of the boxes were old book mailers and envelopes. In another box were book jackets from discarded books. The jackets were still colorful and might be useful for the picture file. In one corner was a stack of papers, pamphlets, and handouts from the past three state library conferences.

As Marion, a third-grade teacher, cautiously peeked around the corner, Marty looked up. "Is it safe to come in?" quizzed Marion. The last time Marion had visited, a stack of old newspapers had tumbled off a shelf and onto her feet. "I'm trying to find books for my students to read on the history of Hispanic people in the southwestern United States. It seems to be a difficult topic to find appropriate material on." Marty thought for a moment and then remembered a session from last year's library conference. After searching for about ten minutes, nothing relevant was found. "Maybe," thought Marty, "it was longer than two years ago." After looking through five years of state conferences, Marty decided that a personal contact might be better than written material anyway. Looking in his Rolodex, Marty found three names for the district bilingual center and three different numbers. As personnel changed, Marty had written the new names and numbers and also continued to keep the old names and numbers. They might be useful some day. Three phone calls later, Marty discovered that a fourth person was now in charge of the bilingual program. This name and number were duly recorded along with the other three, but since the only space left was in the middle of the card it was difficult to tell whether this was the new name or one of the old names.

Marty likes casual organization. Everything is equally important and equally useful; it all might be needed one day. The casual tendency is particularly strong among librarians. It is an emotional drain for librarians who prefer this approach to dispose of any item. Nevertheless, in this age of information explosion it is becoming more and more necessary to be selective in retaining materials. Below are some strategies that may make it easier for casual space users to keep the most important items and begin to discard less used materials.

Marty attended a meeting of a local environmental group and discovered that services were now available for recycling paper, cardboard, plastic, glass, aluminum, and many other things that the library stored. Even though it was difficult to get rid of the boxes, papers, and envelopes stacked on top of the cabinets and shelves, Marty knew the materials would not be wasted. With money the library received for recycling, Marty created a fund to purchase plants for the library. Two positive results were achieved: items were removed from Marty's office, and the library environment was improved by the addition of green plants.

While reading a time management book, Marty found three other techniques that might work. The bottom drawer of Marty's desk was designated as the "Possibly Useful to Someone" drawer. Marty dropped items into the drawer until it was filled. Once the drawer was filled, Marty had to remove and recycle old things before he could put something new in. Marty also discovered that if items for recycling were left in the library office it was tempting to remove things from the pile and store them in the library. Marty solved this problem by having recycled materials removed daily by the custodial staff. Then he established a schedule where once a week he removed two items from the file cabinets and recycled them. This was a small but important step for Marty. It helped reduce the emotional impact of discarding items by making it part of a regular routine.

Case of the Clinging Carpet

Robin

Robin's office walls were striking and colorful. Posters created by students during their library lessons filled every available space. Poster paints were lined up on the window ledges and on top of cabinets. Drawers overflowed with projects that students and Robin had made together. In one corner was a plastic sack filled with rubber stamps and multiple colored stamp pads. Mail was stacked on the desk, the floor, and the chairs. Sometimes it was difficult to tell if a stack was mail or another project, as flecks of paint had fallen onto all the stacks. In one corner sat a heap of carpet samples. Underneath the samples were a VCR, a video camera, and a tripod. Below the video equipment was the case into which it all fitted.

Robin arrived, flung her coat on top of a pile of mail, and pulled the VCR, camera, and tripod out from underneath the carpet samples and headed out the door. Students were to present the results of their research projects on the Revolutionary War. Each group had to prepare a news report about the War. Reporters would interview students who took the characters of people such as George Washington or General Lafayette. Other reports centered around daily life, such as making hasty pudding or dipping candles. Robin was in charge of organizing and videotaping the projects. As the taping began, she realized the camera was not working properly. Upon investigation, Robin discovered that strands of fiber from the carpet samples had become entangled in the camera's mechanical parts. The camera would have to be sent for repair and another would have to be borrowed before the projects could be recorded.

Robin has adopted a creative approach. This indicates a person who is too busy to be concerned with how things are organized. The creative librarian values creativity and spontaneity. This person finds it too difficult and time-consuming to bother with sorting, filing, and straightening. Time spent doing those things is time taken away from helping students make collages, create books, or develop HyperCard stacks. Presented below are simple techniques to help people with creative characteristics spend the minimum time attending to details and the maximum time doing the important things.

The broken camera was the last straw for Robin. No one at work had complained about the state of Robin's office. They were happy with the products that students created and with what students learned, yet Robin realized that something needed to be done. Having equipment break down due to something as silly as carpet fibers was annoying. Robin also knew that any complicated system would not work, so she decided to allot ten minutes a day for straightening. Ten minutes was not much time and would not interfere with any project or activity. Robin realized it was going to be difficult to consistently organize and tidy and that a reward system to reinforce organized behavior would be useful. She created a long list of entertaining and creative activities. After ten minutes of straightening or organizing, Robin would choose one activity as a reward. Finally, she developed a simple sorting and filing system for mail. All catalogs, fliers, and promotional materials were dropped into a large colorful box. Students, faculty, and staff could browse the box and take what they wanted. Personal correspondence and important mail were put into an in-box. All other mail was put in the trash without being opened. Robin was not concerned about missing something in the mail, but with dealing with mail as efficiently and quickly as possible in order to get onto the really important things.

Tony

Case of the Gray Day

Even though the sun was shining as Tony walked into the library office, it seemed like a dreary day. The gray steel desk was prepared for the beginning of a new work day with calendar turned to the appropriate page, priority To Do list on the right side of the desk, and the first tasks prominently placed in the middle of the desk. Neatly labeled gray boxes with the materials necessary to complete today's To Do list were stationed on the gray steel shelves behind the desk.

Just as Tony begin reviewing the specifications for purchasing new CD-ROM drives, the telephone rang. The children's librarian was on the other end: "A group of senior citizens is presenting an impromptu puppet play for the pre-school program today. Would you like to attend?" Tony's answer was instantaneous. "No, I am working on a priority matter at the moment." As he replaced the gray handset of the telephone, Tony felt a brief moment of regret. It might have been an interesting program.

Returning to the CD-ROM specifications, Tony filled out a standardized checklist on each of three different models, compared the results, and decided to purchase the second item. He filled out the purchase order request, provided in the work file, and placed it in the gray plastic out box.

Tony proceeded throughout the day, completing items in To Do order priority, including working for two hours on the circulation desk and two hours on the reference desk. At the end of the day, Tony took 15 minutes and prepared the desk for the next morning by changing the calendar, placing a new To Do list on the right side of the desk, and placing the first task in the center of the desk. As Tony began to leave the office, a piece of the gray carpeting held the door briefly. As Tony was dislodging the obstruction, a library patron walked by and complimented him on the great pre-school program today. Tony's last thought on leaving the building was that the day had been almost as dreary as the morning had promised.

Tony has a functional approach to space use. The coordinated office of gray furniture, gray accessories, and gray ambience provides the least visual distraction, does not show dust, and is easily replaceable because it is a standard office color. The office is organized for efficiency and productivity. Often an overzealous functional approach can result in reduced flexibility, failure to take advantage of spontaneous activities, and a general feeling of weariness. Provided below are some strategies for increasing flexibility but still maintaining an overall functional environment.

The next day Tony was browsing in a local office supply store and noticed a desk just like the one in the library office. However, it seemed more interesting and inviting. A closer inspection revealed that the gray desk was complemented by red accessories. It was bright and colorful. Tony's first response was, "How inefficient. Those would really show the dust." Then Tony remembered how dreary the office had seemed yesterday. Perhaps it would be possible to make a few minor changes and brighten things up just a bit. Since the items were on sale, Tony decided to try new red trays and red shelving boxes for the To Do materials. If they showed dust too badly, they could always be replaced.

Tony had also been considering the senior citizen presentation. The library had received many compliments and comments, yet Tony had no knowledge of what had occurred or why. He decided to be more open to spontaneous events and choose to do something unexpected or new once a week. In addition, he decided to try to have one day a month when no To Do or priority list was planned. These two changes helped open Tony to more spontaneous activities and provided for more flexible opportunities.

When Tony left the office that day, the air seemed clearer and the sky brighter. A library patron asked if Tony was attending the repeat performance of the puppet play tomorrow. Tony's response was immediate, "Yes. I want to see what you all have been talking about."

PUBLIC SPACE

The stories of Jan, Lynn, Robin, Jerry, Marty, and Tony describe how librarians' space use preferences are reflected in their use of personal space and how techniques can be applied to work with personal space preferences. Librarians are also responsible for public space. Public space is used by many people with many different space preferences. The personal choices of a librarian may or may not be appropriate for the group of people who use the library. It is important for librarians to be able to separate their personal preferences from the needs of their users.

In creating and using the public space in a library it is important to recognize that the space is used by many people. No matter which organizational system predominates in the management of the library environment, someone will not like it. It will not match someone's values of how space should be used. This problem is of particular concern for librarians who prefer visible or casual space use. These two styles do not match the predominant belief that public spaces should be neat and well organized.

TIME MANAGEMENT EXERCISE 9

Conflicts in Space Use Preferences—25 minutes

1. Review the space use preferences and identify the one most like your own. It does not have to be a perfect match.
2. Review the space use preferences and identify someone you know who has preferences which are significantly different from yours. Choose the preference which the person most closely resembles but it is not necessary to find a perfect match.
3. How do you perceive the work of this other person? Do you believe they are doing things the wrong way? Are you tolerant of the differences in your ways of organizing space?
4. How do you believe this other person perceives your way of organizing space? Are they tolerant of the differences?
5. If you discover conflicts or lack of tolerance think of one area where you could change either your perceptions or the other persons.
6. Brainstorm three or four ways to resolve the conflict and try one soon.

Another common problem is a conflict in space styles with administrators or coworkers. If a supervisor prefers formal space organization and the librarian has a visible space use preference, conflicts are possible. It may become the librarian's responsibility to negotiate with a supervisor about the need for different space use in the library.

If a librarian prefers an invisible approach and coworkers prefer materials to be visible, there is also a potential for conflict. Those who prefer visible space use may say: "The library is boring. It does not have any interesting pictures or posters." To you the empty space and clean environment is an inducement to work. To the person with the visible preference it is a barren wasteland, an emotional desert. Conflicts in space use preferences in public environments will always exist. The time challenge to the librarian is to meet the needs of users, supervisors, and coworkers and still maintain a personal comfort level.

Three advanced procedures for analyzing your time use result in information to change or reinforce your priorities:

Intensive time diary
Single problem analysis
Outside observers

ANALYZING TIME CHALLENGES

In Chapter Two simple procedures for analyzing time use were discussed. They were to identify general patterns of behavior. By using beginning techniques, librarians start to understand what takes time and what typical responses may be. This chapter explores techniques for gathering more extensive information and looking at challenges in more detail. The following section explores three techniques. The intensive time diary records extensive details of day-to-day activities. The single problem analysis provides a method for collecting and analyzing information about a specific time challenge. This process shows librarians how to proceed through a complex analysis of a single important issue. The final technique involves the use of an outside observer to catalog a librarian's time use and interactions.

All three methods require an initial time commitment to collect information and additional time to analyze data. All require the commitment of two weeks to one month to be effective. The resulting information is rich and detailed. The data can be used to revise and change behavior related to time management. It can also be used to understand which uses of time are most effective. Another use is in making management decisions. Data from an intensive analysis can be valuable for justifying new budget items. It may provide significant statistics on peak times of library use where assistants or volunteers could be used most effectively. The results of an intensive analysis may also demonstrate who is not using the library and may become the basis for a promotional program or campaign. The investment of time will be worth the information gained for some librarians. For others, these techniques do not smoothly match their time or work preferences. There is only one way to find out. Read on and try something! Following a definition and discussion of each technique, you will find a brief analysis of different time use preferences and their relation to the technique.

THE INTENSIVE DIARY

The intensive diary is a record of daily activities written at approximately 15-minute intervals throughout the day. It is a labor-intensive task that results in very personal information. Analysis involves sorting through large quantities of information to identify patterns of interaction, time use, and constraints. Questions are generated from analysis of the intensive diary and lead to further analysis or to implementation of specific time management techniques.

Collecting information for an intensive time diary is completed in one to two weeks. Gathering information over time helps identify patterns and relationships. Specific forms for recording information are available through resources such as *J. K. Lasser's Executives Personal Organizer Forms* (Goldstein, 1988) or supply houses such as Day-Timer, Inc. and Memindex. Forms may also be created using a computer data base program such as Filemaker II, Works, D-Base, Fox-Base, or Appleworks. Another technique is to purchase a diary or notebook and write at 15-minute intervals, carefully noting the day and time before each entry (see Figure 7).

Once a form has been chosen, the next step is to consider the type of notes to keep. Complete details provide the basis for more complex analyses. Consider the following questions as you write your diary entries:

- What did I do?
- Who did I do it with? Include names, positions and numbers.
- What did I say?
- What did others present say and do?
- How did I feel? What were my reactions: emotional? physical?
- What did it appear that others felt? What were their nonverbal reactions?

If collecting information to answer all those questions is too overwhelming you may wish to focus on gathering one specific type of data. For example, write down only what you did or write down only how you felt. While this will decrease information collected, it will also increase your ability to analyze and draw conclusions (see Figure 8).

Once the information has been collected, analysis can proceed in several ways. If you created a database and entered the information into a computer, consider a frequency analysis. How often do certain people's names appear? What are feelings such as joy or dissatisfaction related to? You may search for interruptions and identify the patterns within which interruptions occur. A computerized data base program may be unnecessary as you can do the analysis by hand, simply

FIGURE 7 Intensive time diary form

Time Diary

Day ____________ Date ____________

7:00
7:15
7:30
7:45
8:00 (continued in this way throughout an entire work day)

adding up occurrences to obtain frequency counts. Do certain activities result in consistent feelings? Below are some of the questions about which an intensive diary can provide information:

- Who do I spend most of my time with?
- What activities take up most of my time?
- What activities make me feel positive?
- How much time do I spend thinking and planning?

Many other questions could be answered or tentative questions created from keeping an intensive diary.

Intensive diaries are generally kept for one to two weeks, but they can be kept for as short a time period as three days. Collecting detailed information over time helps to establish patterns and relationships. Some advantages are extensive knowledge about what was done, notations on feelings and attitudes, and a feeling of accomplishment for tackling a difficult time task. Another advantage is that noting information in the diary may increase awareness of what others do and say. One disadvantage is that it is an intense and time-consuming process. Keeping the diary may actually change everyday behavior. It is also easy to lose motivation with such an intense task.

The intensive diary activity may be repeated over time. For

FIGURE 8 Categorical time diary form

Date____________

Time	Who involved	What accomplished	How did I feel

example, keep an intensive diary for a week. Implement time management strategies and techniques for three to six weeks. Then keep an intensive diary for another three to five days. Compare the results from the second diary with the first. Note changes, positive results from the new techniques, and other items of interest. Continue with time management and try the intensive diary a year later. This strategy provides insight by crystalizing moments in time.

Librarians whose time management has achiever tendencies will like this technique. It is detailed, requires intense concentration, and results in many projects to work on. The disadvantage for achievers is that it will show the flaws in their work schedules. It is important for achievers to use the intensive diary as a helpful tool rather than a critical examination. Librarians who fall into the conceptualizer category most often find this technique onerous. It is detailed, time-consuming, and results in many small pieces of information. Other analysis procedures will be more to their liking. For precisely the reasons that conceptualizers dislike the intensive diary, organizers enjoy it and can use the technique successfully. It draws on their major strengths of attention to detail and organizational procedures. Risk takers, multitaskers, and information gatherers may use the technique with mixed results. The intensive diary offers no thrill or emotional roller coaster for a risk taker. There are no time constraints and no rewards for completing one. Only external motivation, such as a directive from a supervisor with time limits, would make the intensive diary interesting to a risk taker. Multitaskers will find the intensive diary fascinating at first, but will become distracted quickly. Writing in the diary may remind them of something else they are interested in, and they will be off to other things. Information gatherers may find the diary to their liking in writing the entries, which require little decision making. Conducting the analysis, however, means making multiple decisions, and at that point the diary may become difficult.

SINGLE PROBLEM ANALYSIS

The intensive diary concerns breadth of issues related to time use. The single purpose analysis focuses on one area. The identification of a single challenge may be the result of using one of the simple analysis procedures suggested in Chapter Two or it may also derive from an intensive time diary. A personal realization or problem can also generate a single problem analysis. In the single analysis, information is collected in response to questions generated by the problem rather than collecting information to generate questions. The final product is definition of the problem, analysis of how the problem is currently being addressed, and recommendations for future changes. The process of conducting a single problem analysis begins with three questions:

- How do I define the problem or challenge?
- What do I currently do related to this problem or challenge?
- What do I want to do differently about this problem or challenge?

As you proceed with analysis, answers may change as information is gathered and priorities and needs are articulated. Answers and questions are interconnected. As you define the problem, you gather further information. Some of this information may change the problem definition. Redefining the problem may make it evident that only a small portion of the problem need be worked on now. As you answer the three questions posed above, you may create further questions and increase the scope of the analysis. Narrow the scope to a few tasks and concentrate effort if necessary. The process is somewhat like a reference search that identifies narrower terms or broader terms to help solve problems. Presented below is a sample analysis of a single time challenge discussed in Chapter One: the impact of technology on libraries and librarians.

Case of Time versus Technology

Bernie, a junior high school librarian, decided to analyze the problems of technology in the library. He began by changing the question, "How do I define the problem or challenge?" into one directly related to technology. Then he developed the components necessary to define the problem.

Bernie's question was, "How do I define the problem of integrating technology into my library media center?" In response, he decided that the first step was to create a list of technologies considered part of the problem. Bernie's list included these technologies: computers, CD-ROMs, online public access catalogs (OPACs), laser disks, microfiche and microfilm, established teaching technologies (e.g. filmstrips, overheads, cassettes), telephones, local areas networks (LANs), electronic encyclopedias, online or CD data bases, video components (e.g. VCRs, cameras, video display devices), and scanners. When Bernie felt comfortable with the technology list, his next step was to clearly state the problem.

Bernie's first attempt at a problem statement read, "Technology seems like it will save me time and will help students learn better, but it seems impossible to know everything and it costs a lot of money." After thinking about this for a while and talking to some faculty members, Bernie created the following question: "Are the perceived benefits of professional time savings and increased student learning worth the professional time investment and financial costs?" Analyzing this question, Bernie realized that there were contradictory statements being made in terms of time management. The first half of the question said that technology saved professional time, while the second part of the question implied that technology used professional time. Focusing on this conflict, Bernie resolved to collect information about how much time was taken up interacting with technology.

In the next phase Bernie looked at the question, "What do I currently do related to this problem or challenge?" for a detailed analysis of a time problem. The revised question stated: "What do I currently do related to the problem of how much time technology takes or saves?" From the initial list Bernie created a checklist of technologies available in the junior high school library. For a week, Bernie kept track of how much time he spent using, repairing, or learning about the technologies. At the end of one week, Bernie had collected the following information. (See Figure 9.)

In a 40-hour week, Bernie was amazed to discover he spent 30 hours interacting with technological devices in some way—approximately three-fourths of his time. Even though much of the time spent using the technology was also spent teaching or working with students and faculty, this was a significant emphasis in one area.

Bernie decided it was time to work on the final question, "What do I want to do differently about the time technology takes in the library?" Was it appropriate for Bernie to spend three-fourths of his time interacting with technology? After considering this question, Bernie realized that the issue was not exclusively the time spent with the technology. Different activities were involved in spending time with technologies. Some of those activities were more important than others. Bernie decided to concentrate on two areas: one for increasing the effectiveness of time spent with technology and the other for decreasing the time spent with technology. In this way Bernie addressed both issues in the original question.

To increase the effectiveness of time use, Bernie chose to focus on the activity of keeping informed about new technology ideas and changes. Since it was impossible to keep up on everything, Bernie created a plan for making more information available in a more effective manner. Bernie asked three other librarians in the same area to form a support group. Each librarian keeps up on a specific area of technology. Every two months at a breakfast meeting they share the expert knowledge they have accumulated. They distribute responsibility for learning about new technology and gain an opportunity to discuss the use of technology in libraries with other professionals. Other librarians from the area are now asking to join the group.

Bernie was uncomfortable with the amount of time he spent on the telephone and saw this as a possible area for reducing time spent with a technology. For two weeks, Bernie kept a careful log of all phone calls. The length of time, purpose, and caller were listed. A brief analysis showed that phone calls from sales representatives took up approximately two hours per week. Sales calls are now screened through an office

FIGURE 9 Time spent with technology in a typical week

Technology	Using	Repairs and Maintenance	Learning About
Telephone	4 hr		
Old things	1 hr	3 hr	
OPAC	4 hr		2 hr
CD-ROM	2 hr		3 hr
Video	1 hr	2 hr	
Computer	2 hr	2 hr	2 hr
Misc			2 hr
TOTALS	14 hrs	7 hrs	9 hrs

Total Hours for all activities = 30

switchboard, whose operators take names and phone numbers. Bernie returns calls only to representatives whose products are of interest to the library. Conversations with sales representatives are kept to a five-minute maximum through the use of a timer.

Bernie continues to examine other technology issues that surfaced as a result of the detailed problem analysis. He was surprised, for example, at the amount of time spent on repairs and maintenance of technology. If that much time was really needed, a part-time technician should be considered for the next budget cycle. Another option was to increase regular maintenance from once to twice a year, thus minimizing emergency repairs. Bernie is also studying OPAC use to discover if self-instructional materials could reinforce instruction provided for large classes. Bernie is convinced that, since significant time is spent interacting with technology, it is important to follow through from knowing to doing.

Addressing a single time problem requires focus and critical analysis. The conceptualizer, who concentrates on general patterns, may be successful using this technique. It applies their strengths to analyzing a general time management issue. Achievers may find this analysis overwhelming. They may spend too much time and energy following through on all questions and issues generated. This may also be a difficult analysis procedure for information gatherers. It requires extensive decision making in all phases of the analysis. Multitaskers and organizers may or may not use this technique effectively. Its emphasis on looking at a problem in many different ways will appeal to multitaskers, but they will need to follow through and carry the strategy to a conclusion to be effective. Organizers may appreciate collecting the details, but avoid the necessary conceptual analysis. Risk takers will use the technique especially well if it is connected to a deadline such as a grant proposal, budget cycle, or presentation to administrative personnel.

The advantages of the single problem technique are that it creates a plan to solve a specific problem. It develops definitions, range of the problem, and future directions. The disadvantages are that focusing on a single problem can make it seem overwhelming and unsolvable. Spending a significant amount of time on a single problem may also mean that other problems are not attended to. When engaging in this technique it is critical to choose a problem that has significant impact on all areas of the library and will benefit the maximum number of people and result in significant changes.

OUTSIDE OBSERVATION

Outside observation requires another person to watch and take notes on your behavior. The purpose is to provide a detailed view of what you are doing and how you are accomplishing it. An outside observer is not intimately involved in the content and may more carefully document behavior. Outside observers may also record nonverbal behavior for all participants. Having an outside observer describe space use also helps to identify personal preferences, which can stand in the way of seeing the environment clearly.

Observations by outsiders may be conducted in different ways. They may sit in the library and take notes for a specified number of days. They may follow the librarian around and record activities, conversations, and interactions. The observer may also focus on certain questions or issues, such as those raised in the intensive diary. Different observers may take notes at different times. Instead of taking notes, the outside observer might use a checklist of behaviors. The directions given the outside observer will influence what the librarian learns and what the observer does. It is important to discuss with the observer in advance the purpose and methods to be used in the observation.

Observers may be drawn from many areas. Immediately

available observers include library assistants, clerical staff, and volunteers. They regularly participate in library activities and should complete observations with little disruption of the normal schedule. On the other hand, their library experience may make them less objective; they may not see with fresh eyes. In school settings teachers are another source of observers. This allows teachers the opportunity to find out what librarians do. On the other hand, their only open time might be their preparation period. Using one teacher per period per day might result in a variety of observations. In public library settings a colleague from another library could be asked to observe. This could provide needed information and also provide the observer with ideas for different techniques in their library. An assistant principal in a school or a regional supervisor in a public library might also be appropriate. These people might gain a broader perspective of what occurs in your library and might also be able to invest a significant length of time on the task. However, it could turn into a formal or informal evaluation process. Not only would they observe your behavior, but they might make judgments about that behavior and enter them into a personnel file. This could be either positive or negative.

Observers may also be drawn from outside the immediate library environment. A good source of observers is college of education or librarianship students. This could be beneficial to both parties. The students would observe and record in detail the activities and responsibilities of librarians. The librarian would receive information from people interested in the job but with no vested interest in the organization. There may also be researchers interested in conducting an ethnographic study of librarian's work. If this option is available, it provides the most detailed and extensive evaluation. Ethnographers are trained observers and analyzers, and the results of such a research study would be useful to your library and to the profession.

Analysis of observational data, particularly that compiled by another person, must be approached carefully. There is a potential for conflicts in values and interpretations. Asking observers to provide a summary of observations might be a useful technique. Another appropriate technique would be to thank observers for the data but not involve them in the analysis. When looking at observations written by others, it is important to distance yourself from the information. Try not to take the observations personally. Look for patterns and relationships of activities that work and those that need to be improved. Your purpose is to find ways to focus on the positive and to decide what activities to change or eliminate.

This analysis technique can be valuable for examining how your use of time appears to an outside observer. It can result in startling and sometimes dramatic changes in the way you manage time. The result is somewhat like observing yourself on videotape for the first time. Incredulity about how you appear to others may result in significant behavior changes.

Outside observation is a useful technique for multitaskers and organizers. Multitaskers may have difficulty focusing sufficiently to use more time-intensive analysis techniques. An observer removes this problem from the control of the multitasker. Often organizers need the broader context that can be provided by an outside observer. Information gatherers and risk takers may also appreciate the use of an outside observer. Reading carefully the results of their particular preferences may help increase their awareness of how to manage time differently. Observation may or may not be appropriate for a conceptualizer. If they receive a general summary, they may find it quite valuable. Dealing with the vast quantity of detail to create an overall pattern might be difficult for conceptualizers. Achievers will probably avoid this technique as it has too many evaluative components for the achiever's comfort. They already evaluate their performance with critical awareness. Because the observations of others may reinforce their own beliefs that they do not do enough, it can be a high risk activity for achievers.

One advantage of using an outside observer is that as a technique it is not intrusive on personal time and allows the librarian to engage in a normal routine. Observers are also more likely to objectively list and categorize the time the librarian spends doing certain activities. The disadvantages are that someone willing to undertake the activity must be found, their presence may be intrusive, and their ability to accurately record behavior is based on trust. They can record such things as what you do, who you do it with, details of conversations, and notations of body language from which some feelings can be inferred. They can not detail actual feelings. Combining outside observation with a simple personal diary could help minimize this problem. Another disadvantage is that most people can carry out intensive observation for no more than a day or two. Only a trained ethnographic observer could carry out a long-term, detailed observation.

Using observations to graphically demonstrate to colleagues, supervisors, board members, or administrators can improve understanding of library problems and issues. It can also involve a certain degree of risk taking. However, if you are willing to take the risk, the benefits can more than justify the cost.

TECHNIQUES TO ENCOURAGE TIME MANAGEMENT

Managing paper is an essential area where librarians can use encouragement and appropriate techniques. Paper management has both personal and public components, as did the space usage discussed above. Personal paper management and public paper management may result in different techniques and approaches. A general context for managing paper includes disposing, sorting, filing, and evaluating. This section provides specific techniques. Some will be useful now; some will be useful in the future; some may never be used. When reading through this section, choose techniques of interest. Write them in a notebook or remember them and implement at least one this week. Start the process of translating from knowing to doing by using one new technique immediately.

MANAGING PAPER

Manage paper in both your personal and public spaces effectively!

Paper management reflects the basic dichotomy of a librarian's job. Managerial paper and service-related paper may need to be organized differently. Managerial paper is more likely to accumulate in a librarian's private space. Organizing managerial paper will reflect a librarian's personal preferences. Service-related paper consists of public materials such as periodicals, pamphlets, newspapers, catalogs, and promotional materials. Organizing service related paper will reflect traditional library cataloging and filing techniques (i.e., American Library Association [ALA] filing rules, Sears or Library of Congress subject headings, and more contemporary electronic indexing systems). Managerial systems respond to personal preferences, styles, and organization. Service-related systems require standardized methods of organization and structure. This section focuses on managing administrative and personal paper. It examines the relationship between personal and public paper management, placing emphasis on creating personal systems that work with established public systems.

Managing paper is an element of space usage and can be handled in many ways. Presented below is an array of techniques for managing paper focusing on four critical areas: disposing of paper, sorting paper, filing paper, and evaluating paper. Take notes or remember ideas that seem appropriate or interesting. Consider creating variations or adaptations to suit your space management and time management preferences.

An essential paper management technique discussed by most books on time management is minimizing paper handling. This means sorting, filing, or working with a piece of paper the fewest times possible. Skopec and Kiely describe the outcome of failing to address this issue in the following way, "Even a few pieces [of paper] hang in the system and cause enormous backlogs because we end up going over and over them again and again" (1991, 74). Each time you look at a piece of paper you are making a decision. Putting the paper aside to review at a later time is a decision. Making a postponing or reviewing decision increases the time spent on this one issue. Multiply these decisions by the number of pieces of paper and mail a librarian handles everyday, and you can see that much time is used postponing decision making. In order to streamline the paper handling and decision making process, consider the following ideas.

Dispose of paper

Dispose of as much paper as possible on the first handling. Barbara Hemphill in *Taming the Paper Tiger* (1988) calls this process managing "the art of wastebasketry." She recommends using a large wastebasket. In her experience people are more likely to throw things into a large wastebasket than into a small one. In addition, she indicates that 80 percent of the paper we save is never actually used. Save time and effort by throwing out rather than storing and find an appropriate recycling program. The decision to throw out paper will be easier if the paper is being recycled. Use the wastebasket, trash can, or recycling bin as the first step in your paper management system. The more things in the trash or recycled, the less left to sort and file.

Create a sorting plan for items left after the wastebasket and recycling bin have been used. Most sorting systems result

Create a sorting plan

from one of two basic approaches. With the first approach categories are established in advance. Paper is placed into predetermined stacks based on the categories that have been developed. As an example of the second approach, Susan Silver (1991) suggests that the most important component of a sorting system is the goals to be achieved. The goals direct the sorting process and the categories chosen. The second approach requires sorting papers over a period of time. The resulting stacks then dictate categories used in the future. Whichever scheme is chosen should allow for changes in paper received and goals to accomplish.

For a librarian, sorting through one day's mail might involve ten, 20, or 30 decisions. The easier a sorting system is to implement, the less time the process will take. Three examples of sorting systems from the simple to the complex are provided below.

- A simple sorting system for librarians might be two stacks: personal paper and public paper. Personal paper could be organized using the librarian's style and public paper put into appropriate technical places for processing through a standardized system.
- Another sorting system might be to organize paper by what is to be done with it: needs action, read, file, send elsewhere. For librarians, this system might integrate personal and public materials. The advantage, however, would be that the librarian knows the next steps to be taken by the action file the paper is placed in.
- A more complex system might involve sorting by type of material (e.g. catalogs and promotional flyers, periodicals and newspapers, pamphlets and materials for the collection, letters and correspondence, business and financial). While this might take longer initially, it could smooth decision making at later stages. Clerks, volunteers, or assistants might be able to handle many of the stacks of paper through already established library policies and procedures.

File before it falls over

Sorting and filing are interdependent processes. Some librarians do sorting and filing simultaneously. This may take longer initially but result in paper being handled one less time. Personal paper may be more easily sorted and filed simultaneously than public paper. In libraries public paper usually requires another level of processing after the sorting stage. Develop a filing system that responds to your way of working. If you can effectively manage a complex filing system, then implement it. If you do not have the time or inclination to carry through an intricate filing process, then devise a simple system. Use broad general categories and anticipate that sometimes you will need to look through a number of items before finding the one you want or need.

Evaluate paper regularly

Paper that is not filed may require further evaluation. Some time management experts recommend dividing the unfiled paper into priority folders. For example, as you look at a piece of paper, decide if this is an A, B, or C priority. Place all As in one folder, Bs in another, and Cs in the third. Complete the items in the A folder first. If you still have time, tackle the B folder, and so on. Another recommendation is to organize paper by what needs to be done (i.e., urgent matters go in one folder or stacking tray, papers to be read in another, and papers related to certain topics such as purchase requests in another).

Another necessary form of paper evaluation is an ongoing process for reviewing filed materials. If left by themselves, files will continue to grow until they fill all available space. Since 80 to 90 percent of filed materials is never used again, it is important to create a system for evaluation and disposal of filed materials:

- One technique is to note, when a piece of paper is filed, how long it should be maintained. This information could be handwritten in an upper corner (e.g., "Throw out in January, 1994").
- Another technique is to assign a portion of the filing cabinets to be evaluated on a regular and rotating basis. For example, in January of each year, publishers' catalogs are reviewed and old items disposed. In February, financial files are evaluated. In March, evaluate lesson plans or planning documents. In April, evaluate photocopied articles A-M. In May, evaluate photocopied articles N-Z. In this way, over the course of a year or two, all files in the office are reviewed and unused items disposed of.
- A third technique is to review a file folder each time it is used and dispose of unnecessary items.
- A fourth technique is to dispose of old materials when new ones are filed. For example, dispose of the old

TIME MANAGEMENT EXERCISE 10

Developing Paper Management

10 minutes per day for one week

1. Choose one area of paper management to concentrate on: disposing, sorting, filing or evaluating. Choose an area you believe causes you a time management problem.
2. Analyze the way you currently handle this aspect of paper management. Pinpoint exactly which part of the disposing process, for example, creates the problem. Can you easily dispose of catalogs but have problems with letters in envelopes?
3. Devise a strategy to strengthen your problem areas. Consider the techniques discussed above, review other time management resources or create your own unique strategies.
4. Implement your chosen technique for ten minutes each day during the next week.
5. Evaluate the results. Was the problem more difficult than you initially thought? Did everything work reasonably well? Did your motivation decrease?
6. If the technique worked well, continue it. Repeat the process and add another technique next week.
7. If the technique did not work, try another or choose another area to work on. You may also decide to go on to another exercise or area.
8. Whatever the results, reward yourself for trying.

publishers' catalog when the new one arrives. Too many library files have backlogs of materials that should have been disposed of as new information took its place.

Dealing with mail, stacks of paper, and backlogs of personal and professional files requires concentration and decision making. It is not a process that should be undertaken when tired, depressed, or anxious. Trying to manage paper under these conditions reduces effectiveness, increases time expended, and results in further feelings of anxiety or depression. Hemphill summarizes the process for creating an effective paper management system in this way: 1) eliminate unnecessary paper; 2) avoid generating unnecessary paper; 3) establish a location for essential paper; 4) create a method of easy retrieval of paper (1988, 25). This book adds a fifth component to the system: evaluate paper on a regular basis.

Fires lead to dire consequences. Get them under control immediately.

FIRES, INTERRUPTIONS, AND TIME MANAGEMENT

How do you balance immediate needs, short-term problems, and long-term commitments? This section addresses simple approaches to identifying and dealing with immediate needs. People often refer to dealing with immediate needs as putting out fires. Because the underlying assumption when discussing fires is that things are out of control, methods for retaining control are addressed in the section on putting out fires. The relationship between time management problems, interruptions, and fires is also discussed, and short-term solutions to these problems are identified. Chapter Four presents a mechanism for formal planning that looks at long-term issues and their relationship to day to day activities.

PUTTING OUT FIRES

The definition of a fire is critical to understanding how to control and put out fires. If you define a fire as any interruption and treat all interruptions as if they were potential crises, then life will be filled with continuous drama. If you define a fire as a crisis situation that requires immediate response in order to reduce the possibility of escalation and real damage, then you are approaching fires differently from other types of interruptions (Mackenzie and Waldo 1981, 61). Responses to typical interruptions were discussed in Chapter Two. This section uses the second approach for defining a fire—a crisis situation that demands immediate response. It also discusses techniques for identifying, controlling, and fighting fires.

Fires can be identified by the direness of the consequences resulting from not immediately attending to the problem. The most emphatic level of consequences would be if not taking action would result in harm or physical injury. If you or someone else would die or be physically injured, then, of course, the problem must be attended to immediately. This is truly a fire. It is a conflagration. While this may seem an extreme statement, it also serves to create a point. To truly be a fire, the problem must be highly significant and must be attended to immediately. Get that five-year-old down off the ladder! All other problems should receive some time and thought before action is taken.

Fires may also have significantly negative social or personal results. If not attending to the problem immediately meant the loss of your job, that would be a significantly negative result. Losing friends or the respect of colleagues or students might also be significantly negative social consequences. The threat of job loss is a fire. The extent of the fire would be gauged against your need to retain the job. Social consequences will vary in intensity for different people. For some people, losing a friend or losing respect could be a dire result; for others, it would be annoying; for still others, it might be a minor irritant. You will want to carefully evaluate the problem and perhaps take some immediate steps toward solving it.

Situations that are emotionally uncomfortable or result in feelings of dissatisfaction may or may not be considered fires. If you do not attend to the problem will you feel angry with yourself or with someone else? While these feelings of anger may be justifiable, the problem may not represent a true fire. Using assertiveness techniques can be particularly valuable with problems at this level. Assertiveness can help you to articulate clearly why the problem will not be handled immediately. Assertive "no" statements or assertive statements limiting involvement can reduce your anger. Other emotions that can be addressed using assertiveness techniques are feelings of self-defeat, awkwardness, and dissatisfaction.

Some consequences clearly indicate that a problem is not a fire. For example, even though the consequences may seem significant, if the problem can actually be fit into a schedule and dealt with as time permits, it is probably not a fire. If the problem makes you feel that you have not done your job properly or that you should have done better, then the problem is most likely not a fire. Another indication that something is not a fire is if you feel you really should be doing something else. These may be important problems; they are not fires. Important problems can be dealt with by using the techniques discussed throughout this book and in other time management books.

Below, as a review and a way to help differentiate between fires, time management problems, and interruptions, is a list of activities that might fall into each of the categories:

- *Fires are*: threats to job security, threats to program security, threats to personal security, threats to student or patron security and health, significant threats to emotional well being.
- *Time management problems are*: mail sorting and handling, too much to do, requests from supervisors, requests from peers, requests from students or patrons, deadlines, meetings, equipment maintenance, personnel who do not do their job properly, overscheduling, not leaving time for emergencies or interruptions, interesting things you do not have time to do, library scheduling conflicts, book orders, budgets, cataloging, problem students, problem teachers, problem administrators, problem library users, problem supervisors.
- *Interruptions are*: trivial details needing immediate responses, an unexpected visitor, continual phone calls, broken equipment, immediate information needs, student discipline, reference questions, salespeople.

Once you have identified a fire, it is important to take action. The consequences to either you, your program, or someone else are severe. Analyze the situation. Decide on the minimum action necessary to bring the fire under control. If you discovered a real fire in your library trash can, your action would be to smother it, or perhaps, to use the fire extinguisher. This could bring the fire immediately under control. Begin to create your own fire extinguishing techniques. Clear communication of expectations and responsibilities is one of the most effective fire extinguishing techniques for librarians.

You also may discover that someone else could handle the problem more efficiently or effectively. Pass the fire on, unless inaction would cause harm. In the case of problems that could result in imminent, bodily harm, physical injury, or severe mental distress, take action immediately. If a real fire in the library was out of control, the first step would be to evacuate the facility. Then you would call fire fighting professionals to finish the job. If you encountered a student or a patron in severe emotional distress, your first action might be to find out what was wrong. You might be able to talk some problems through with the person, while others would require professional counselling or guidance. Be willing to know your limits and request help from other professionals.

With problems whose consequences might jeopardize your personal or social stability, try to identify the severity of the problem. One critical question to ask yourself is, "Can anything actually be done?" For some problems, there may not be an action that is appropriate for you to take. Look for all possible solutions, but do not punish yourself over problems that you cannot successfully address. With personal and social fires, it is important to gather all pertinent information. Many difficult social situations are the result of the report of one person, who while believing that he or she has clearly clearly articulated the issue, may have misunderstood. Before taking action in these situations, gather data. Solicit opinions from two or more people. Take the time to think through responses thoroughly and completely. For further techniques for dealing with problems that have personal or social consequences consider the section on self-esteem in Chapter Four.

CREATING A TIME MANAGEMENT SYSTEM FOR TRANSLATING KNOWING TO DOING

This chapter discussed advanced analysis procedures, examined paper management in detail, and looked at the differences between interruptions, fires, and time management. Librarians reading this book have acquired knowledge. The next step is to create a time management system to translate knowledge into more advanced doing activities. As before, a recipe is provided for librarians who wish more structure. A less structured set of decision points is provided for librarians who want flexibility in time, choice of activities, and possible outcomes. Use the recipe and the suggestions for a more advanced time management system or create your own system based on your own categories and needs.

Recipe for advanced time management

This system requires a longer commitment in terms of time and energy than the one introduced in Chapter Two. It is for librarians who feel confident they are doing some time management activities well, but who wish to engage in more advanced time management techniques. Set aside one month

TIME MANAGEMENT EXERCISE 11

Putting Out Fires—30 minutes

1. Write down or think of one example from each of the three areas that you have encountered recently: fires, interruptions and time management problems.
2. Write or remember the interruption and time management problem to work on later. If they came readily to mind for this exercise, they are probably areas which are important to you to resolve.
3. Examine the problem you identified as a fire. What made it a fire? What were the significant consequences?
4. How did you handle this fire? Did you give it to someone else who was more knowledgeable? Did you deal with it yourself? How long did it take to bring the fire under control?
5. List three specific things you did to manage the fire.
6. If the same or a similar fire occurred in the future, would you do the same things? If so, then keep these ideas in mind the next time a fire erupts.
7. If you wish you had handled things differently, what other actions could you have taken? List three different ways of handling the fire.
8. Repeat the process for the different types of major fires you think might occur in a six month period.
9. Post your lists of fire prevention/handing techniques somewhere you can see and review them regularly, just as you would emergency fire procedures.

for implementing this advanced time management system. Plan on approximately 30 minutes to one hour per day for practicing your new time management techniques and strategies. Remember, implementing these activities may actually save you more than the hour per day you are committing. With the longer time commitment, it is important to reinforce your efforts with regular motivational activities and rewards.

Day 1: Set aside about 30 minutes planning time. Consider the possible positive outcomes of using more advanced time management behaviors. Make a list of all the things you think might happen if you worked on time management consistently for the next month. Post the three most important outcomes in a prominent location in your office.

Day 2: Choose one of the advanced time analysis procedures. Read through it carefully and make a plan for implementing it for seven days. Schedule when you will work on this analysis procedure each day. Make an appointment with yourself to do this.

Day 3: Begin to gather data for an advanced time analysis. Continue this through Day 9. Review the information briefly at the end of each day and begin to make judgments about what is happening.

Day 10: Analyze the results of your data collection. Use Days 11 and 12, if necessary, to create a written, audio, or video report for yourself of the important time challenges uncovered. Choose a single time management problem to work on for the next part of the month.

Day 13: Choose time management techniques from this chapter, other chapters, or your own experience that you believe will help solve the management problem you have uncovered. Create a plan for implementing these techniques over the next five days.

Day 14: Implement chosen techniques. Continue through Day 19. At the end of each day briefly review the outcomes and consider how you will modify or improve the activities the next day.

Day 20: Review the month. Make a list of the positive changes that have occurred. Make a list of the time management techniques, procedures, and strategies you have used. Which resulted in positive changes or outcomes? Continue using those that worked well. Discard those that did not. If you feel confident about advanced time management, continue on to Chapter Four. If you feel you want more practice, create a two-week plan for continuing advanced time management strategies.

Flexible system for advanced time management

This section suggests a process for creating a time management system but does not prescribe the elements, the time frame, or the range of activities. It is a way for librarians to create plans responding to personal needs and requirements. Consider the five components of a time management system, but only use those of interest to you. Follow the steps below to create an advanced time management system:

1. Establish a trial period in which to practice advanced time management techniques. A minimum of three weeks or a maximum of six would be appropriate. Pick the time frame and fit information from the following into your preferred time limits.
2. Consider the five components of a time management system: motivation, self-awareness, analysis procedures, implementation techniques, and planning strategies. Clearly decide which of these you are interested in implementing. Choose one, none, or all. Make a mental, audio, or written list of those areas you will work on.
3. Choose activities, processes, or exercises to try out during the time frame you have established. Create a plan that integrates these activities into a useful schedule for you. Make regular appointments with yourself to keep focus, energy levels, and commitment high.
4. Keep a mental, audio, or written record of your feelings, responses, and successes. Particularly note the relationships between techniques and successful changes.
5. At the end of the time frame chosen, reflect on the usefulness of the activities, the way they were implemented, and your responses. Create a written, audio, or video record of your progress as a motivational device.
6. Develop a plan for your next steps in time management.

You may choose to repeat this process. You may go on to Chapter Four for time management long-term planning information. You may choose to focus on one of the new time management books (e.g. Bliss 1991; Davidson 1990; Mackenzie 1990; Webber 1992; Winston 1990). You may choose another book, tape, or process entirely. If time management is still important to you, make a plan to extend the commitment and make the transition from knowing to doing on a regular basis.

4 FOCUSING ON THE FUTURE

Focusing on the future requires long-term commitment to:

- Integrating work and home
- Increasing self esteem
- Keeping appropriate records
- Managing people
- Creating long-range plans

This chapter examines time management approaches to planning for the future. Earlier chapters covered simple strategies for developing commitment to change and for moving from knowing to doing. Chapter Four looks at long-term approaches for motivation, self-awareness, time analysis, implementation, and planning. These approaches help develop a personal vision and implement professional long-term planning. The motivation section discusses integrating work and personal life. An appropriate balance between professional responsibilities and personal needs is most likely to result in sustained motivation. The self-awareness component of self esteem in relationship to assertiveness is discussed. Record keeping is explored as a long-term approach to time analysis. Time management techniques for managing people within the librarian's service role are reviewed. Strategies focusing on strategic and tactical methods for organizational planning provide focus for the planning section. Exercises and examples are included to illustrate concepts. A method for creating a complex time management system with long term planning components completes the chapter.

Integrating your personal and work life can help increase the benefits of time management

- Balancing for priorities
- Enhancing relationships
- Matching personal values
- Acknowledging health issues

INTEGRATING TIME MANAGEMENT INTO WORK AND PERSONAL LIFE

Your professional life is less likely to be successful if your personal life is not also satisfying, and your personal life is less likely to be satisfying if your professional life is not also successful. This integration of the personal and professional does not come without conscious decision making and planning. Integrating personal activities and professional responsibilities is a method for focusing on the the future. Work and personal life will be more satisfying when you do things that have long-term meaning. Understanding time is not something left at the workplace. Your relationship to time carries over into all aspects of your life—work, home, family, and play. Feeling happier, calmer, and more successful at work will have an effect on the way you feel at home and in your personal life as well. Learning to understand and work with time can be as valuable for your family and friends as it is for you. This section looks at ways to integrate work and personal life by creating balance and acknowledging the effects of personal problems and health issues.

CREATING BALANCE BETWEEN WORK AND PERSONAL LIFE

One of the most important aspects of integrating work and personal life is creating a satisfying balance between the two areas. Balance does not mean that each area is necessarily equally represented; it means choosing to do what is most meaningful to you. Balance is internal and based on your needs and hopes. Balance comes through conscious choices about work life and home or personal life. It is a way to build awareness of yourself, family, friends, and others who influence your personal and social well being. It can help you examine time to create meaningful contexts. When short-term conflicts occur, they can be resolved more easily when you look at the balance you wish to create. Integrating work and personal life will improve your self-esteem, your feelings of personal worth, your relationships with others, and your management of time.

Time is a way of valuing activities!

Time management is a way to identify balance points that are necessary and important to your satisfaction. Balance can be created through prioritizing, planning, organizing and decision making on a professional level. It can also be created through understanding how work fits into personal life. Your work should reflect your values. Time is a way of placing value on activities. Time engaged in doing something implies that the activity is valuable. Is this true of the things you do in your library? Do you spend time on things you believe make a significant difference? If your honest evaluation tells you this is not true, then reexamine what you do.

If you are dissatisfied with work, frustrated and unhappy, there may be a mismatch between your use of time and your personal values. Time management is a way to create balance between personal beliefs and professional priorities. If people were to guess what you believe to be important from watching how you spend your time, would you be satisfied with the results? Would you say, "Yes, filing cards, shelving books, and replacing burned-out equipment bulbs is the most important contribution I can make."

Examine the way you spend your time as an outsider would. What would you think about a person who spends their time the way you do? What would you infer about their values and priorities? If this does not match up with your self-image and beliefs, you may be unhappy or frustrated. Your personal satisfaction can be increased by bringing the time you spend into line with your personal beliefs.

If this is not a problem and you are convinced you spend time doing only the really important things, but that there are more important things to do than there is time, then another approach to balance is necessary. You might be an achiever (see librarian's time use in Chapter Two). Achievers like to have things done perfectly. Because they take extra time on each project to be certain that things are perfect, they may be able to do only a few things. This will frustrate achievers because they believe they should be able to do more. However, they will never be able to do enough at the level at which they believe they should achieve.

Even librarians who are not achievers may be trying to do too much. No matter how much you wish to, you cannot do all the things that need to be done. One person probably cannot bring peace to the world, solve the hunger crisis, and create a major symphony. It is not possible to do everything. It is possible to do things that you like, enjoy, and that contribute to making the world better. Realizing that your standards may be unnecessarily high is difficult. It is hard to give up perceptions of quality and quantity in order to concentrate on fewer activities and issues. It is even more difficult when everything you do is important and substantial. You must make decisions about which of the worthwhile activities will result in the greatest benefits for yourself, your workplace, your family, and your friends. Difficult choices about what to keep and what to minimize must be made to create a sense of balance. The following books provide more detailed approaches and differing philosophical viewpoints on creating balance between personal and professional life: Davidson 1991; Eyre and Eyre 1987; Hunt and Hait 1990; Lakein 1973; Schlenger and Roesch 1989. Time management can be a journey of self-discovery, not simply a mechanical undertaking to squeeze

TIME MANAGEMENT EXERCISE 12

Priorities and Time Spent—20 minutes

1. Make a list of the five things you do which take the most time. You may focus on work time, personal time or both. Try to consider categories which capture the essence of what you do. You may make daily estimates or weekly estimates, whichever seems most reasonable to you.
2. For example, a school librarian's analysis of five work time categories might look like this for an average day:

Instruction	5 hours
Equipment problems	1 hour
Interruptions	2 hours
Teacher conferences	1/2 hour
Personal	1/2 hour

3. Put your completed list aside and do something else for an hour or longer.
4. Make a prioritized list of the five things you would like to spend most of your time on. Be certain that this list parallels the construction for the first. If you made a list of five work time categories for your first list, do the same for this one.
5. The librarian above might have created the following list:

    1—instruction
    2—teacher conferences
    3—helping students
    4—planning
    5—personal

6. Compare the time spent with your wish list of priorities. How might you make them more closely match if there are major discrepancies?

more minutes out of each day so you can do more things which may not be valuable.

PERSONAL PROBLEMS AND HEALTH ISSUES

For a working librarian, discussing personal problems in

Personal problems affect work.

Work affects personal health and well being.

the context of time management may seem unacceptable. There are strong social pressures to believe that personal problems should not interfere with job performance. It is precisely this myth that creates time challenges on the job. Personal problems do affect work performance. This conflict needs to be recognized and factored into the allocation and management of time. Personal problems or illness will affect the time it takes to complete activities and the effectiveness of decision making. The more severe the personal problem or illness, the greater the impact will be on job performance and time management. It is important to recognize the relationship. During times of personal problems or illness, set realistic goals and priorities. Adding to stress with excessive expectations of yourself will help neither work nor personal life.

The major time challenge to librarians facing personal problems or illness is the need to decrease the amount of work and to set realistic temporary new goals and priorities. Once the crisis has passed, situations may be reexamined. Stress has a strong influence on decision making abilities. It clouds judgment and results in feelings of guilt, inadequacy, and lack of confidence. You may feel that someone is behaving in a way that is insulting to you, or you may be rude to another person unintentionally. Under conditions of stress or illness, decision making is much more difficult. It takes more time and more energy. Social relationships, accuracy, and level of performance may suffer when you try to do too much. You can hurt yourself and others by not acknowledging the impact of personal problems and illness on your job performance.

You can also hurt your personal and social relationships by not recognizing the impact of job problems and stress on your family, home, and personal life. Stress and frustration created by too much to do and not enough time on the job will have an impact on your personal life. You may spend more time on the job trying to catch up. You may go home tired and irritated. You may forget to pay the monthly electric bill and return at the end of the day to find your home in darkness. You may "blow up" at a relative or friend for no good reason. You may become distracted and more accident or sickness prone. When you begin to confronting the realization that you can not do all that there is to do, you may become even more frustrated. Increasing self-esteem and assertiveness are two ways to minimize the effects of job stress on your personal life. If you feel better about yourself, it will be easier to relate to family and friends positively.

SELF-ESTEEM AND ASSERTIVENESS

The two previous self-awareness issues of a librarian's time use and space preferences were specific and resulted in the ability to take immediate action. Self-esteem is a more complex self-awareness issue and requires greater time commitment and emotional involvement. Understanding self-esteem is a long-term project, but can result in significant life changes.

Self esteem is both self respect and self confidence

Self-esteem consists of two parts: "a feeling of personal competence and a feeling of personal worth." (Branden, 1987, 6). Personal competence, sometimes called self-confidence, is the belief that we can accomplish the things we set out to do. It is our belief in our own abilities, knowledge, and intelligence. Personal worth, sometimes called self-respect, is the belief that we are deserving of the confidence placed in us. It is our belief in our own fundamental goodness. People may have high self-confidence and low self-respect or low self-confidence and high self-respect, or some elements of both. Self-esteem is the combination of these two parts.

Twelve ways to increase self esteem

Self-esteem and assertiveness are interrelated. Each influences the other. Using assertiveness techniques can help enhance self-esteem, and increasing self-esteem positively affects assertive actions. People who have self-confidence believe their actions will result in positive consequences. Janette Caputo in the *Assertive Librarian* (1984) brings together the two concepts of self-esteem and assertiveness. She indicates that assertiveness can be an important component in developing self-esteem. Assertive behavior can lead to increased feelings of self-worth, which in turn lead to further assertive behavior and a constructive cycle is developed. Caputo suggests the following 12 ways for librarians to increase their self-esteem (1984, 70-72):

- Talk to yourself, using positive labels and self-statements.
- Agree when people compliment you.
- Remember compliments when you are having a difficult day.
- Reinforce positive self-statements with a specific action.
- Make a set of catalog cards with your positive self-labels on them.

- Make two public positive self-statements each day.
- Turn negative self-statements into positive statements.
- Reinforce yourself each time you change a negative to a positive.
- Give compliments.
- Provide yourself with mental reinforcement when faced with anxiety laden situations.
- For heavily ingrained habits, mentally shout STOP IT!!
- Use visual imagery as a reinforcement.

Each of the preceding ways to increase self-esteem will also have a positive influence on your ability to engage in assertive activities. As your self-esteem increases through practice, it will be easier to say no, to set limits, and to make difficult decisions. Use the exercise below to practice positive actions for both self-esteem and assertiveness.

SELF-ESTEEM IN THE ONE-PERSON LIBRARY

Case of Sagging Self-Esteem

You name it, Stacy was it: the librarian, the clerk, the manager, the cataloger, the instructional designer, the accountant. Stacy was the administrator of a one-person library, and Stacy was becoming more and more frustrated. Each day the list of things to do got longer and the list of things done was shorter. There never seemed to be a time when everything was finished. When one project was completed, another was still underway and a third should have been started the day before. Things always seemed to be behind schedule. Requests were always emergencies because there was no time to complete them. The more Stacy accomplished, the less confident she felt because there was always more to do. No matter how hard she worked, it was impossible to complete everything that needed to be done.

People coming into the library started to notice changes in Stacy's behavior. When Stacy first started the job, she answered questions cheerfully and completely. Sometimes she sent follow-up notes along with a personal query about how the materials had worked out. After a few months on the job, Stacy looked startled when asked a question, and sometimes snapped out answers like, "Look in the card catalog," or "It's on the second shelf by the potted plant." Chris, an avid library user, saw that Stacy was sitting hunched over the computer with a perpetual scowl and a clenched jaw and asked if something were wrong. Stacy replied, "No, I'm just really busy. I'll talk to you later." Sometimes Stacy would interrupt a

TIME MANAGEMENT EXERCISE 13

Increasing Self Esteem

10 minutes per day for one to two weeks

1. Choose one of the self esteem techniques listed above. Remember that increasing self esteem requires a longer commitment. Two weeks would show more positive results
2. Focus for ten minutes each day on increasing your self esteem. Consciously practice the technique you have chosen.
3. Be aware that you are working to increase your self esteem. Think positively about what you are doing.
4. At the end of the time period chosen, decide what you will do next to continue increasing your self esteem.
5. Consider purchasing a self esteem cassette tape to listen to as you drive or walk to work.

user's question in the middle to answer the telephone, leave the telephone off the hook to answer the caller's question, and upon returning to the desk wonder why the caller could not wait and the patron had left.

The demands of the one person library had brought Stacy's self-esteem to an all-time low. One day the pressure became too much and Stacy decided to take time to relax and read. While browsing through a professional periodical, Stacy discovered an article on self-esteem. After two weeks of trying out one of the techniques, she started to feel a bit better. There was still just as much work to do, but Stacy realized that focusing on what she had not done brought no rewards. Stacy chose to concentrate on more positive accomplishments, to accept the limitations on service imposed by a one-person library, and to acknowledge that lack of self-esteem is beneficial to no one.

It was still not easy, but Stacy's self-respect and self-confidence increased day by day. This improved the overall library environment, and library users began to feel comfortable in the library again. They were still not happy when Stacy said, "No, I do not have the time or the resources to do that for you." Stacy's more assertive statements initially caused some discomfort. As she persisted, however, the library users came to more clearly understand the limitations of a one-person library. In the short term, Stacy took extra time to explain the problems and to prioritize services. In the long term, both Stacy and the library users gained from her improved self-esteem.

LONG-TERM ANALYSIS PROCEDURES

The application of specific analysis procedures, such as those described in Chapters Two and Three, is more likely accomplished in a few days, or a month or two at most. These analysis procedures may provide initial information for long-term planning and development, but cannot sustain the effort. Since their implementation does not generally extend over long periods of time, other methods for information gathering must also be employed. The analysis procedures from Chapters Two and Three can be used to develop the categories of information to be collected through long-term record keeping. An activities checklist might indicate that certain activities occur so rarely they do not need to be part of a regular record keeping chart. It might be more appropriate to briefly describe the Leap Year Fine Amnesty procedure than to check on a chart each time it occurs. Other activities from the checklist may indicate the need to keep detailed time and participation data as a foundation for increased budget to support growing needs. Consistent record keeping will supplement more intensive analysis procedures and provide basic information for decision making over longer periods of time.

KEEPING RECORDS

When considering time management, one of the first images that may come to mind is making lists, writing in diaries, and filling out forms. This type of record keeping predominates perceptions of time management. The predicted results are a tidy office, papers in their proper place, tasks completed appropriately, and leisure time to think and plan. Keeping the appropriate records is often seen as the answer to time problems. While lists, schedules, charts, graphs, records, and file systems can be helpful—and even indispensable—they are not time management. They are the raw data for the analysis of time management issues and the resolution of time management problems.

Time management is an internal commitment to do the things that are important. The many techniques that can help foster internal time management are part of the analysis process of time management. They alert you to problem areas; they serve as memory aides; they provide checks and balances to priority issues. Record keeping helps identify patterns over time but, to be truly useful, the records must be integrated into a long-term planning process. Record keeping, as a long-term time management tool, must be directed by your personal needs for information to help you develop life goals and priorities and by your library's long-term need for information.

Do you already keep these personal records?

How you keep personal records will depend on your time use and space preferences. Librarians with organizer tendencies or a casual space preference may want to keep everything. All records—from old To Do lists to notices on the back of envelopes—would be interesting to librarians with these two styles. The conceptualizer or the librarian with the functional space use preference might not want to keep any personal records, but for different reasons. Since these are personal records, it is your choice about what to keep and for how long. Keeping these records will not provide solutions to time management and decision making problems, but they are signs along the way to point out directions and possible alternatives. What kinds of personal records can be helpful to keep?

- To Do lists
- Daily priorities lists
- Quarterly objectives
- Daily diary or log
- Long-term goals and objectives
- Activities that you engage in and how long they take—activities checklist
- Underestimates of the time necessary to complete a task
- Energy cycles
- Interruptions that are the most annoying or the least important
- Behavior changes over time
- Lists of subject headings for your personal files
- Addresses and phone numbers
- Regularly reoccurring activities

TIME MANAGEMENT EXERCISE 14

Keeping Personal Records

15 minutes per day for two weeks

1. From the types of personal records listed above choose the records you already keep. Add others you keep that are not on the list.
2. Write down two uses you would have for each of the types of personal records. For example, if you chose to keep track of how you delegated tasks. One use might be to find out who you delegate to on a regular basis. The other use might be to find out which type of tasks you delegate.
3. Analyze the results. Are these records that would be worthwhile to keep over a long period of time, e.g. a year or two. Do they provide substantive information for justifying budget requests, planning long range programs, demonstrating the range of your work activities?
4. Examine your personal records on a regular basis, keeping those that contain substantial information and that can easily be kept up over a long period of time.
5. Consider the types of personal records you do not keep. Would some of them be more worthwhile for providing substantive information?
6. Eliminate personal records that are no longer useful and add techniques which might be of value.
7. Use these records as a foundation for creating both personal and professional long range plans.

- Jobs delegated to others
- Questions which could not be answered
- Common and reoccurring problems
- Interactions with colleagues
- Serendipitous activities
- Spontaneous changes in direction

Only you can know which personal records are worth keeping and for how long. Use the exercise below to help identify which personal records you currently keep and how useful they are. Then use the second part to develop a plan for keeping personal records in the future.

Keeping professional records is addressed in all administration texts for libraries. The obvious records include circulation statistics, patron use, budget figures, and collection strengths and weakness. The less obvious records include items that cross over from the personal to the professional category. Your personal list of phone numbers or office file subjects may also have professional value. Carefully examine the relationship between the typical administrative records necessary for the smooth functioning of a library and personal records.

If you have time or space use preferences that do not mesh well with keeping personal records, you will need to modify this for keeping professional records. Record keeping is important to professional decision making, and appropriate information must be gathered for successful long-term planning. Keeping records is a major responsibility for librarians. It is a time-intensive process to keep records, interpret records, and translate records into reports and other usable formats. Librarians need to examine both personal and job created records to determine their value and the importance of the time expended.

MANAGING PEOPLE

This section considers a personal approach to managing people. It looks at relationships with people as part of the librarian's service responsibilities. Five strategies for managing people in this environment are discussed: delegating, motivating, coordinating, communicating, and instructing. The focus is on the types of interactions librarians use to work with the people they serve. It is meant to develop a cooperative environment between librarians and library users. This section differs from traditional approaches to managing people in that it looks at the service role rather than the managerial role. Information on using management techniques for personnel issues and management responsibilities can be found in the following books and tapes: Blanchard 1990; Blanchard and Oncken 1988; Blanchard and Oncken 1989; Mackenzie 1990; Oncken 1984; Shipman, Martin, McKay and Anastasi 1983; Winston 1983; Winston 1989.

Sharing responsibility for the library and at the same time developing self esteem in others can be done through:

- Delegating
- Motivating
- Coordinating
- Communicating
- Instructing

MANAGING PEOPLE THROUGH SERVICE

As discussed in Chapter One, the conflict between a librarian's service and management responsibilities results in conflicting time demands. The service component of the job requires librarians to be available on demand. This section looks at how to manage service time through managing relationships with the people involved. Managing people in this context consists of five types of activities: delegating, motivating, coordinating, communicating, and instructing. Each activity has implications for managing time and managing people. Being able to manage the use of time appropriately during these interactions is essential to librarians for long-term effectiveness.

Delegation is a key element in time management and is always considered as part of the management component of a librarian's job. Delegation also has a significant role in the service component of a librarian's job. Librarians need to manage relationships with the people they come in contact with in their daily work. A service provider's focus is on managing the relationship rather than managing the people. The expected outcomes are responsible people who share common values and ideas about what can be accomplished in a library environment. Delegating in this context means asking people for their help when you need it. This could include asking patrons to retrieve back issues of periodicals from the stacks or teaching students to check out their own books. It is a sharing of responsibility rather than the formal delegation of a business environment.

Motivation of others, particularly library users or students, can increase a librarian's available time and increase satisfaction with the library. Motivated people are interested in doing things for themselves and are more rewarded by internal feelings than external requirements. Librarians can help library users develop motivation by providing them with the skills to use the library independently and effectively. They do this through providing positive role models and through the three other activities listed below: coordination, communication, and instruction.

Coordination of people in a library is not only the job of the supervisor or administrator. Librarians can improve use of the library through coordination of efforts and appropriate use of scheduling procedures. Coordination of efforts means that library users or students and faculty are involved in decision

TIME MANAGEMENT EXERCISE 15

Delegating Responsibility—1 hour

1. Find a management book or cassette tape which has a section on delegation. Either a time management resource or a regular business management resource will do. Read or listen to the section on delegation. Any management resource will do, they all handle delegation in much the same way.
2. Choose a problem you would like help on in the library that someone else could do. Perhaps library users could shelve their own books. Perhaps teachers could help check out books to students. Use your imagination.
3. Write or remember two delegation techniques which could be of help in solving this problem.
4. Using a cassette tape player, practice what you will say to ask someone help you solve the identified problem. Incorporate the delegation techniques into your requests.
5. Practice with the tape recorder until you are confident.
6. When you are ready, ask for help. Keep thinking about the problem. Eventually through improved self confidence, you will be able to share responsibility on a regular basis.

making, from new paint for the storage closet to the information skills curriculum to purchase of a video collection. It allows library users to share the responsibility of choices for their benefit. It helps the librarian understand how changes can be made to best fit the needs of the user. Coordinating schedules, equipment checkout, and other repetitive tasks can significantly reduce a librarian's expenditure of time.

Communication is essential in relating to people in all areas of life. Communication involves a vast array of techniques from written to oral activities. Listening is one of the most difficult communication tasks. Librarians need to develop their abilities to listen effectively. Many problems can be averted through carefully listening to requests. Confusion or dissatisfaction in the voice of the speaker should alert the librarian to ask probing questions. Gathering more informa-

TIME MANAGEMENT EXERCISE 16

Coordinating Efforts—90 minutes + travel time

1. Visit another library. Quietly sit for thirty to forty five minutes. Do not do anything. Observe closely what is going on around you. (Choose a time when the library is relatively busy.)
2. Take notes on what you saw, heard, felt or experienced. You may write the information or record it. Particularly note areas where you thought people could benefit from working together more closely.
3. What would have helped things run more smoothly? Better communication? Better motivation? Better instruction? Better delegation?
4. Create a plan for helping the librarian coordinate one activity in the library to save time.
5. Ask the librarian you visit to help you by visiting your library and creating a plan for you.

tion or understanding the users request more clearly can help save a librarian's time.

Case of the Missing Fish

Recently a librarian was asked by a third grader, "Do you have any books on fish?" When the librarian asked, "What kind of fish?" the student replied, "I don't know, just fish!" The librarian was listening carefully. It was obvious the student did not realize that there were different kinds of fish and materials about fish could be shelved in two different sections of the library. Books on fish such as sharks would be in the five hundreds but books on tropical fish would be in the six hundreds. The librarian continued the conversation by asking the student, "What are you going to be doing with the book?" He discovered that the student had goldfish at home and wanted to "put a lady and a man goldfish together so they could have babies." The librarian's carefully listening and responding to the student resulted in a satisfied student who found a book on goldfish. The librarian was also satisfied because as part of the search process the difference between the Dewey five hundred numbers and the Dewey six hundred numbers were made very relevant to the student.

For school library media specialists, instruction is perhaps the most time-consuming portion of managing people. Sched-

TIME MANAGEMENT EXERCISE 17

Instructional Time—1 hour

1. Briefly analyze how much time per week you spend in direct instructional activities. An approximate estimate is fine. For public librarians consider time spent telling library users how to do something as instructional time.
2. Briefly analyze how much time you spend preparing for instruction. Again an approximate estimate is fine.
3. For school library media specialists be certain to include time spent teaching faculty or staff in addition to students. For public librarians include time spent showing assistants, other library staff or volunteers how to do things as part of your time commitment.
4. What proportion of your typical work week is spent in instructional activities?
5. Are you satisfied with the amount of time and the activities that are part of your instruction?
6. Consider your emotional as well as intellectual responses to the previous question.
7. If necessary, use the techniques described in the strategic and tactical planning section to create long term and short term goals for improving or revising instruction.

uling instruction, delivering instruction, reinforcing instruction, and reviewing instruction take a significant portion of a school librarian's time. Managing faculty and students within the instructional environment is a significant problem for school library media specialists. Public librarians also create and deliver instructional messages. These can be as simple as a sign indicating how to use the photocopier or as complex as a demonstration of how to retrieve information from the online public access catalog. While public librarians deliver little formal instruction, they are constantly engaged in an informal learning process. Both short-term and long-term approaches to managing people through instruction are necessary. The most effective method for dealing with long-term instructional needs is through a strategic plan (discussed in the planning section of this chapter) with accompanying tactical plans (also discussed in the planning section of this chapter).

Taken together, delegating, motivating, coordinating, communicating, and instructing provide the foundation for librarians to manage their service role more effectively. These techniques can be used to motivate library users to share responsibility for management. Librarians who ask people to help them manage the library are developing strong and reliable supporters. Library users who are involved in the decision making and management process become more aware of the library's priorities and needs, and also improve their independence and self-esteem. Managing people in this sense benefits everyone.

PLANNING AND TIME MANAGEMENT

As with other activities in the library, librarians engage in both personal and professional planning activities. Personal planning activities have been discussed earlier in this book in terms of doing the right thing, moving from knowing to doing, putting out fires, and in the sections on short-, medium-, and long-term planning for beginners. Each of the sections on developing a time management system is an example of a personal planning strategy, as are the motivation sections from each chapter.

Two types of planning interact to help librarians develop goals and priorities:

- Strategic plans for the future
- Tactical plans for the present

This section focuses exclusively on long-term planning for professional success. The techniques and strategies described are most useful for developing long-range library plans and the accompanying specific programs. Long-range planning is one of the most important professional techniques for time management because it clearly sets direction and establishes priorities. It also helps identify areas where personal goals can be integrated into professional needs. The differences between strategic and tactical planning are examined. This section also discusses processes for implementing strategic planning and provides specific examples of tactical plans. The section concludes with a method for integrating strategic and tactical planning into an overall process for long-range planning.

Strategic planning can be divided into five parts:

Missions
Policies
Outcomes
Plans
Revisions

STRATEGIC PLANNING

The strategic plan sets parameters for decisions. It provides the framework for tactical planning to create procedures, budgets, and day-to-day activities. Strategic planning should take place at the highest administrative level possible. Involving administrators, library board members, community leaders, staff, and district or regional personnel results in a strategic plan based in community needs. It provides justification for future expenditures and establishes philosophy and policy. The outcome of strategic planning is written policies and goals for libraries that reflect organizational policy, philosophy, and objectives.

A five-step approach to strategic planning consists of the following activities:

1. Create a mission statement
2. Develop policies and long-range goals
3. Predict possible outcomes
4. Create long range plans
5. Evaluate, review, and revise.

Each step builds on the previous step and integrates into the succeeding step, creating a continuous and interactive process.

Create a mission statement

Determining the mission of the library is the first step in strategic planning. Mission statements answer the questions: What purpose does the library serve? Why does it exist? Review and revise previous mission statements at this stage. Creating mission statements requires the input of representatives of library boards or school administration, library users or faculty and community members. In a process called "Zero-In," Craig Lundberg (1984) lays out a six-step technique for formulating mission statements:

1. Announce the meeting time and place

2. Outline the purpose and importance of the meeting
3. Ask participants for their views about the mission statement
4. Review and synthesize the statements
5. Develop the mission statement
6. Discuss the technique.

This technique is cost- and time-efficient, provides common experiences for decision making, and functions as a model of teamwork for creating other policy statements.

Develop policies and long-range goals

As a second step in strategic planning, develop both general policies and specific long-range goals. Policies direct the creation of goals and long-range options and set the parameters for predicting possible outcomes. Long-range goals form the framework for creating strategic plans. Policies and long-range goals are the foundations for making changes in libraries and planning for the future. They establish priorities, set future direction, and provide a framework for tactical plans. Clearly stated policies and long-range goals are essential for strategic planning to be effective. After creating written policy, develop long-range goals. Strategic goals identify the basic purpose of new directions and coordinate with policy and mission statements. Long-range goals set the stage for creating long-range strategic plans.

Predict possible outcomes

Look to the future and attempt to predict possible outcomes as the third strategic planning step. Consider changes in community or student populations and changes in library staff or school faculty. Will the library grow or face reductions and budget cuts in the future? What new educational theories and advances will affect schools? What instructional methods are going out of fashion? What new management theories or budgeting processes will affect public libraries? Is the technology market for libraries static or expanding rapidly? Answering future questions is the most difficult step in strategic planning. It requires choosing from among possible futures and taking risks. It is important to realize in predicting possible outcomes that no one can be completely accurate about the future. Your goal is to make the best estimate possible with available information.

Create long-range plans

Once a mission, policies, long-range goals, and a future forecast exist, libraries create long-range strategic plans as the fourth step. These plans form the basis for designing activities, timelines, and budgets. They set the direction for achieving long-range goals. Strategic and tactical planning are the outline and the details. Strategic long-range plans create the general categories, areas, and direction. Tactical plans are the activities and details. Once a long-range plan has been created, it is advisable to secure a formal commitment of cooperation from library users or faculty members, school administration, or community members and the library or school board.

Evaluate, review, and revise

Evaluation, review, and revision are critical to the success of strategic planning. Concrete, measurable, and ongoing evaluation and review should be part of each component of the strategic planning process. In addition, an overall revision and evaluation should occur at regular intervals. Evaluation, revision, and review insure that changes in the environment are incorporated into all aspects of strategic planning.

When evaluating, apply both formative and summative techniques. Formative evaluation examines activities and processes as they occur. Participants in strategic planning may keep diaries of their activities and discuss strengths and weaknesses of the process and the outcomes. Interviews will elicit specific responses to areas of concern. Observe implementation activities for further formative information. Compile the impressions, specific answers, and observations into recommendations for ongoing changes in goals or plans. Summative evaluation is generally formal and occurs as a summary activity. Committees look at strategic goals and plans and ask if these are reflected accurately in the tactical plans. Implement formal objective and subjective measures such as surveys, observations, and checklists.

Revise and review strategic plans on an annual basis. Make certain they still reflect current conditions. If necessary, change plans or policies to reflect current needs. Be aware of external pressures influencing the educational climate. The revision and review process keeps strategic plans for new technology viable. A technology can disappear from the educational marketplace and a replacement appear in a single year.

Riggs (1984, 65) believes, "The process is more important than the plan itself. The plan is a closed-end instrument, while the planning process is more sustaining. Once the initial five year plan is developed, it should be carefully reviewed during each subsequent year. Goals and objectives attained during the first year should be 'rolled off' the plan, existing strategies either recycled or discarded. The strategic planning team readapts its thinking and generates new strategies."

TACTICAL PLANNING

Tactical plans come in a number of variations:

- Program plans
- Project plans
- Standing plans
- Single use plans

Tactical plans are the mechanisms for managing problems. Tactical plans direct the organization to achieve overall goals created in strategic plans. They provide the means to an end and include programs, budgets, procedures, and rules. Tactical plans, also called action plans, direct the actions and activities of participants. When a tactical plan is developed each of these steps should be included:

- Conduct a needs analysis
- Establish measurable objectives and expected outcomes
- Create activities and identify needed resources
- Set a timeline for implementation
- Develop a budget
- Evaluate for effectiveness in meeting goals and objectives.

Needs analysis helps clarify the problems and sets the parameters for objectives to be developed. Objectives and outcomes delineate what will occur and what participants expect to gain. Activities and resources influence budgetary needs and time constraints. Evaluation reflects the success of the plan and projects possible changes for future plans.

Different methods and types of tactical planning exist. The types of tactical plans particularly applicable to libraries are: program plans, project plans, standing plans, and single-use plans. Program plans and project plans are larger in scale than standing plans and single-use plans. Program plans generally are the direct outcome of strategic long-range plans and are broad in their scope in terms of both time and expenditures. Project plans are a single component of a program plan and usually address one specific problem or issue. Standing plans are used for long-term repetitive activities, while single-use plans are for one-time-only problems. Together program, project, standing, and single-use plans provide an array of planning activities for libraries.

Program plans

Case of the Cooperating Libraries

A program plan is a large-scale complex plan created to achieve a specific goal or set of goals established during the strategic planning process. For example, a library goal may state: "Technology will be used to further cooperative collection development among the libraries in the Western Region." Possible methods for implementing this goal are diverse. The Region could distribute all library collections on CD-ROM. It might convert collections to MARC format, create a CD-ROM of holdings, supply each library with CD readers, personal computers, and laser printers, and then update the CD's quarterly. The region might meet the same goal by creating and circulating a data base of library's special subject areas. A telephone request would result in a needed item mailed via the post office. Both methods are programs for furthering cooperative collection development through technology. Evaluations of program appropriateness would focus on identified needs and objectives.

Returning to the example above, assume a region has completed a needs assessment such as that described in *A Planning Guide for Information Power* (AASL 1988) and creates the following objectives for the collection development program.

- Using technology for cooperative collection development in the Western Region will result in: (1) an increase in library user access to materials by providing a greater breadth and depth of information resources; (2) stretching limited resources through a reduction in unnecessary duplication of library materials.

Around these two objectives a program plan is developed

which establishes how to meet objectives, the needed budget, a time line to completion, and an evaluation of the program's overall effectiveness.

Project plans

Project plans achieve objectives within a program plan. Usually short-term components of a program plan, they have specific, concrete, and measurable outcomes. In the example above, the region considering distribution on CD-ROM could have a number of project plans within the larger program. Converting the region's holdings to MARC format is a project within the program plan. Purchasing hardware and software is another project plan within the entire program.

Project plans once created provide specific activities and action steps for library personnel to achieve. Morrisey, Below and Acomb (1988, 63) suggest incorporating the following five factors:

1. The specific steps or actions required
2. Who will be held accountable for seeing that each step or action is completed
3. When these steps or actions are to be carried out
4. What resources need to be allocated in order to carry them out
5. What feedback mechanisms are needed to monitor progress within each step.

The librarian creates the plan and the objectives, but other staff members may carry out the plan. Designate project plans to library assistants, student helpers, or community volunteers for implementation. Involve interested library users in project plans and increase their participation in library activities.

Standing plans

Standing plans are for repetitious actions. They provide guidelines for making decisions about regularly occurring activities. For example, once an automated circulation system is in place, develop standing plans for adding information to the system, providing hardware and software replacements, and upgrading the system. Other types of standing plans could include space planning, staff development, user instructions, and evaluation of effectiveness.

Gathering data for decision making about such issues as new technology is repetitious. A standing plan for data gathering might include these activities:

- Read the professional literature.
- Attend seminars, workshops, professional conferences which address new technology issues.
- Speak with colleagues who are interested in new technologies, who have similar problems or who have implemented solutions.
- Visit libraries with appropriate new technologies.
- Attend demonstrations of new technologies. Write or call for free or inexpensive materials about technologies.
- Create a method for condensing and disseminating information.

Standing plans cover the basic steps of needs assessment, statement of objectives, implementation activities, and evaluation for effectiveness. Review standing plans on a regular basis for relevance and usefulness. A new technology or a new policy development may have made a once-necessary activity obsolete.

Single-use plans

Single-use plans are for unique situations such as budget planning. These plans are generally developed in conjunction with a program plan or project plan. The categories of single-use plans and project plans overlap in some ways. Generally, a single-use plan is more limited than a project plan. It is executed once, completed, and then retired. Weeding the collection may be an example of a single-use plan. The collection weeding plan is created in conjunction with an overall program plan to implement an online cataloging and circulation system. This single-use plan might include selection tools consulted; criteria for removal of materials, including date, condition, and usage; personnel involved; a time line for completion; and disposal of weeded materials.

Other examples of single-use plans could include: (1) the initial budget request for hardware and software to introduce an electronic encyclopedia on CD-ROM, (2) space planning for integrating laser disk players, and (3) rearranging furniture for public-access workstations.

DIMENSIONS OF STRATEGIC AND TACTICAL PLANNING

Scope and time must both be considered when planning:

How big is the project?
How long will it take?

Plans have two basic dimensions: scope and time. The scope of a plan delineates the physical parameters: how much will be included, how much will it cost, and what will be left out. Time planning involves temporal parameters from the short term to the long term. Both strategic and tactical planning include scope and time dimensions for making decisions. Strategic plans encompass a broad scope and long term timelines. Tactical plans are more contained in scope and time but may also include long-term activities.

Generally, the scope of a plan is how much will be included. Scope influences all components of planning, from policy statements at the strategic level to budgets created in single-use tactical plans. When considering the scope of a plan at the strategic level, examine how the plan influences every part of the library. Be certain to include all services, facilities, and users in deliberations for long-term strategic plans. Scope at the tactical planning level examines the impact of details on the overall plan.

Time is the second dimension to consider in strategic and tactical planning. Time runs from the short term to the long term. When considering time in planning, look at activities and actions and the time needed to accomplish them, given certain resources. A short-term project for one library media center could be a long-term project for another. For example, an elementary school library is preparing the collection for automation. Twenty parents volunteer to help inventory, shelf read, and put bar codes on the collection on a Saturday afternoon. At the end of the day, all three tasks have been accomplished using 160 hours of time (20 persons for an eight-hour day). This has been a short-term project for the library media center. In another elementary school, the library media specialist must accomplish all three tasks independently. Two hours per week are assigned to work on the tasks. At the end of 80 weeks or approximately one and a half years, the same tasks have been completed. For the second library, the three tasks were a long-term project. Time is dependent on resources, personnel, and the librarian's management choices.

Integrating strategic and tactical planning along scope and time dimensions can be accomplished in a number of ways. Construct time lines by planning backward from target dates. Show both strategic and tactical timelines on the same charts. Develop budgets from a matrix displaying short-term low-cost activities, short-term high-cost activities, long-term low-cost activities and long-term high-cost activities. Level of funding is only one variable in meeting goals. Integrating strategic and tactical planning means balancing strategic goals and tactical objectives, current and future needs, and internal and external factors. At this point in planning it is important to include contingencies. Plan alternative solutions to identified problems. Build consensus among your community and organizational members through these strategies, budgets, and time lines (see Figure 10).

IMPORTANCE OF PLANNING TO TIME MANAGEMENT

Strategic planning aids decision making by examining future trends and providing long-range goals and plans. Implementation occurs through creating mission statements, developing long-range goals, predicting possible outcomes, creating long-range plans, and scheduling regular evaluation, review, and revision. It is necessary to recognize the interactive and connected nature of strategic planning and tactical planning. Tactical or action plans are the means to achieve the strategic goals. Specific tactical plans are created based on needs analysis, objectives, activities and resources, timelines, budgets, and evaluation. Tactical plans such as program plans, project plans, standing plans, and single-use plans further strategic goals. Through strategic and tactical planning library media specialists improve the use of time and materials.

Emphasis on strategic planning for the future and tactical planning for the present results in both long-term and short-term success. The costs of planning are balanced by the

FIGURE 10 Three scope and time matrix charts

	SHORT TERM	LONG TERM
HIGH COST		
LOW COST		

	SHORT TERM	LONG TERM
Internal Constraints		
External Constraints		

	SHORT TERM	LONG TERM
Strategic Goals		
Tactical Plans		

benefits derived. Strategic and tactical planning turn potential problems into opportunities for increasing awareness, developing understanding, and maximizing the use of time.

CREATING A LONG-RANGE TIME MANAGEMENT SYSTEM

This chapter discussed the importance of integrating work and personal life into any time management system. It explored the development of self-esteem as a method for long-term changes in behavior and increasing personal satisfaction. It also examined the long-term analysis procedure, keeping records, and addressed strategic and tactical planning for developing long-term goals and objectives and short-term strategies.

The final step in this book is to create a time management system over the long-term to provide balance, reinforcement, and continuing motivation. Choose procedures, techniques, and strategies that are most compatible with your natural preferences. This is the most complex level of time management, and it requires depth of awareness and commitment. If you do not feel ready to commit to long-term time management, return to Chapters Two or Three. You may also find a system in one of the books in the bibliography that you prefer to implement. A recipe is provided for librarians who wish help in structuring a long-term time management system. Another flexible approach to decision making is provided for librarians who prefer greater latitude in creating a time management system. Use the recipe and suggestions provided for focusing on the future, or create your own system based on your own categories and needs.

RECIPE FOR LONG-RANGE TIME MANAGEMENT

Focusing on the future cannot be divided into days and weeks, as was done in the two previous chapters. A minimum of four months is needed to implement and practice time management over the long term. Six months to one year is probably a more reasonable time commitment. Any of the techniques or strategies discussed in Chapters Two and Three can be integrated into a long-term time management plan. This recipe provides the skeleton for developing a personal long-range plan; you must flesh out the details. Use the notebook you kept in Chapters Two and Three to choose procedures that fit best with your personal style. If at any point you find yourself loosing motivation or having difficulty, return to an easier task or system such as those from Chapters Two or Three.

Month One

- Choose a motivational strategy to integrate work and life goals.
- Develop planning times and write them into your appointment book for the next four months.

- Write your specific goals for the next three months.
- Develop strategies and techniques for implementing the goals.
- On a single piece of paper draw a picture of your plan and its parts.
- Visualize how you will feel at the end of the four months.

Month Two

- Examine your behavior in relationship to your written goals and your picture. Make adjustments if necessary.
- Use a simple analysis procedure to discover the effectiveness of the techniques you have chosen. Make technique adjustments if necessary.
- Check your assertiveness and self esteem. How do you feel about the changes you have made? Review assertiveness and self esteem techniques if necessary.
- Be sensitive to the behavior and feelings of your coworkers and family. Help them understand the changes you are making.
- Reward yourself for the positive achievements.

Month Three

- Same as month two

Month Four

- Write a brief summary of the changes in your work and family life.
- Make a list of the positive results from your time management changes.
- Identify areas which are still problematic.
- Develop a plan to work on the areas you wish to improve. Include goals and priorities.

FLEXIBLE SYSTEM FOR LONG-RANGE TIME MANAGEMENT

This section suggests a process for creating a long-term time management system but does not prescribe the elements, the time frame, or the range of activities. Consider the five components of a time management system in your deliberations, but only use those of interest to you. Follow the steps below to create a long-range time management system:

1. Establish a time period of commitment for your long-range plan. A minimum of six months to a maximum of two years would be appropriate. The choice is yours. Pick the time frame and fit information from the following into your preferred time limits.
2. Consider the five components of a time management system: motivation, self-awareness, analysis procedures, implementation techniques, and planning strategies. Decide which of these you are interested in implementing. Choose one, none, or all. Make a mental or written list of those areas you will work on.
3. Choose activities, processes, or exercises to try out during the time frame you have established. They should represent the components you are interested in or other time management activities. Create a plan that integrates these activities into a schedule that is useful for you. Make regular appointments with yourself to keep focus, energy levels, and commitment high.
4. Keep a mental or written record of your feelings, responses, and successes. Particularly note the relationships between techniques and successful changes. Also note the responses of others to the changes you have made.
5. At the end of the time frame you have chosen, reflect on the usefulness of the activities, the way they were implemented and your responses. Create a written, audio, or video record of your progress as a motivational device.
6. Develop a plan for your next steps in time management.

You may choose to repeat this process. You may go back to Chapter Two or Three for refresher information. You may choose to focus on a book such as the Hunt and Hait's *The Tao of Time* and eliminate this process entirely. You may choose another book, tape, or method that meets your current needs.

5 SUCCESSFUL TIME MANAGEMENT

Successful time management has strong personal dimensions:

Making changes
Integrating work and self
Living with the consequences
Moving into the future

Successful time management comes from within. It is built on self-esteem and developing a satisfying relationship to time, life, and work. You are the arbitrator of time and success. Motivation, self-awareness, analysis procedures, implementation techniques, and planning strategies will help you achieve the success you wish. However, you must make a commitment to change and follow through with choices and actions to ensure your success. Successful time management also requires working with people to help them better understand your priorities. You must develop awareness of how your changes affect others. When you believe in yourself and your ability to make appropriate choices for the use of your time, you are certain to be successful.

Consequences of time management have positive effects on you, your coworkers, your family and your friends:

Increased proactive behavior
Doing less, feeling better
Why time management works
Resolving inner conflict
Sustaining motivation

MOTIVATION FOR SUCCESS

In the previous chapters, motivation issues related to commitment to change, translating from knowing to doing, and integrating work and personal life were discussed in detail. They provided advice and activities for beginning time management, translating knowledge into action, and focusing on priorities. This section examines three other issues related to motivation: doing less to increase satisfaction, resolving inner conflicts, and sustaining motivation. Doing less to increase satisfaction focuses on the rewards and consequences of decreasing the number of tasks a librarian undertakes and completes. Resolving inner conflicts develops two themes: (1) the conflict which created need for time management and (2) the conflict which results from making changes. Sustaining motivation provides techniques for avoiding negative consequences and enhancing positive activities.

DOING LESS TO INCREASE SATISFACTION

As you have worked on time management throughout this

book, you may have discovered an underlying message that doing less can increase satisfaction. This section provides ideas related to how doing less will increase satisfaction. Conceptually, this is a complex issue. As librarians, we are always trying to do more. Budget cuts, site-based management, and personnel layoffs can provide strong reasons for increasing the number of jobs we do. The perception is that if only we could do more we would not be considered dispensable. The reality is that more jobs done poorly or more tangential jobs done may actually decrease a librarian's perceived worth. Librarians must learn to balance the number of tasks completed with the relative worth of the task both personally and professionally.

How do you prove to a principal or a library board that doing less is advantageous to them? Are they used to you running the popcorn machine, having club meetings in the library, keeping a petting zoo, organizing quilt making activities, and supervising field trips in addition to the normal service and management functions of a librarian? How do you convince them that reducing the number of activities will be beneficial? Are you letting the organization down? Will they decide you are not capable and must be replaced?

With economic and social pressures to increase output, it may be difficult to justify doing less. You may feel guilty saying no. You may feel your livelihood is threatened if you do not agree to every suggestion or job request. Under these conditions, planning becomes essential. Plans help you and others understand why you have chosen to focus on some activities and not others. It helps you understand and stick to priorities no matter what the outside pressures. Doing less when it directly supports planned projects and activities will increase personal satisfaction.

Communicate your priorities for the library program and why they have been established. Supervising club meetings in the library may have to be reduced or eliminated in order to acquire and implement new technologies such as an online public access catalog. A compromise such as allowing clubs to meet in the library, but under other supervision, could be arranged. If the choice is between the time it takes to keep up the petting zoo and time necessary to attend city council policy making meetings or school board curriculum meetings, the meetings may need to take priority. Curriculum development in schools or city council policy making is essential to long-term priorities and goals for libraries. Perhaps the petting zoo could remain in the library, but volunteers could take on the responsibility of maintaining the animals. There simply is not enough time to be effective in all areas. Setting priorities that reflect the needs of the organization, the users, the library program, and the librarian will help you make the difficult decisions.

The library serves an entire school system or community, and your decisions will affect many people. When choosing to do less, involve interested and affected people in the decision making process. If a committee helps to establish strategic planning goals and objectives, it is much easier for you as the librarian to say no to activities which do not fall within the parameters of the long-range goals. Your decisions are seen as reasonable and growing out an overall decision making process, and not random or idiosyncratic. Be true to feelings about what satisfies you and what are important priorities. If your beliefs and those of the majority of the organization come into direct and continuous conflict, consider looking for a position whose philosophy is more compatible with your own. It is not necessary to suffer on the job. The wide-ranging variety of library work and positions allows for many philosophical positions on library service to coexist.

You need to decide the philosophy that will govern your work life. Time management techniques cannot increase the time you have. As a librarian, you really do have more to do than time is available. You have to decide what is important to you. Less rather than more may be the reality. Many things done poorly leave more to do to improve the problems. They reduce self-confidence and self-respect. A few satisfying, successful, and workable things done well may in the long run be of more use to everyone. This will result in greater feelings of self-esteem, which will be more satisfying for you, your family, and the people you work with.

RESOLVING INNER CONFLICTS

Conflict may result from:

- The need to change
- The changes, once made

The resolution of inner conflict is both a reason for wanting to institute time management and a consequence of time management. You may have begun time management as a way to resolve the conflict of too much to do and too little time. By practicing time management techniques and reading about time management you may have discovered other conflicts. For example, changing behavior means being more aware of how others react to you. This may set up an internal conflict. You were reasonably comfortable with the way you behaved in the past; other people's reactions to your established behavior patterns were predictable. By changing your actions you are taking chances. Old habits keep reasserting themselves, and you may feel discouraged. You might find yourself saying things like, "Why go to all this trouble when it takes so much less time to do it the old way? This was supposed to save me time." Learning new skills takes time and commitment. It will result in inner conflicts, but they are new conflicts. The conflicts require an investment, but they can result in better returns. This is why you chose to make a commitment to change. Resolution of the new conflicts will result in personal growth and enhanced self-esteem.

The Tao of Time (Hunt and Hait 1990) suggests another approach to resolving inner conflicts. It recommends removing yourself from the time continuum and looking at the world in a different way. Time becomes an ally, not an adversary. Whether you choose more traditional techniques, Taoist principles, or other methods, there will be inner conflicts both positive and negative. The positive consequences of these conflicts are a renewed vigor and a different perspective on what you do and why you do it. The negative consequences of the conflicts are the difficulties of learning and implementing anything new. Often motivation for making changes related to time wanes quickly. The initial excitement diminishes in the wake of a million and one tasks which need to be finished. Recognizing and working to resolve inner conflicts can improve motivation and help increase the positive consequences of engaging in time management. It can be the first step in sustaining motivation for time management.

SUSTAINING MOTIVATION

Sustaining motivation can be accomplished by:

- Managing negative consequences
- Maximizing positive consequences

Two related approaches can be used to sustain motivation for time management. The first approach examines how to increase and sustain motivation by avoiding negative consequences. The second approach looks at increasing and sustaining motivation through maximizing positive consequences. Both techniques can increase success. They may be used independently or together.

Examining activities or situations to avoid can be an effective way to sustain motivation. No activity is intrinsically bad. However, there may be techniques, ideas, or methods that clash so strongly with personal preferences that they result in failure or reduced motivation. Techniques to avoid are: (1) activities that do not seem interesting, (2) activities that you find boring, (3) activities that are counter to your personal beliefs, (4) activities that do not feel right. When deciding on which techniques to avoid, also consider as a balance that sometimes going against your usual style can help you understand yourself better. You should not choose activities or continue activities if they are not working for you. Anything that causes personal anguish should be stopped immediately. Be honest with yourself about the difficulty level. If it is only uncomfortable but you are seeing results, you might want to persist. Other techniques to avoid:

- Trying to do everything at once.
- Setting goals that are impossible to reach.
- Activities that set you immediately in conflict with everyone in the organization.
- Activities that create chaos or lack of structure.
- Techniques that create too much rigidity at times when you need flexibility.
- Activities that cause you severe emotional or physical distress.
- Techniques that severely cross your own personal style.

Minimizing or avoiding negative consequences is an effective step in sustaining motivation. By planning and being aware of possible problems, you can eliminate or change them. In addition to avoiding negative consequences, it is also important to focus on increasing positive actions and activities.

Maximizing positive consequences can most easily be obtained through increasing proactive behavior. This requires taking the initiative rather than waiting for things to happen. Strategic and long-term planning activities will result in an agenda for how your time is allocated. Having programs and priorities in which you believe strongly will result in more positive actions. To emphasize the positive results of proactive behavior, you will need to give up some activities of lesser priority. Adding proactive behaviors can be balanced with removing reactive behaviors. Presented below are examples of proactive behaviors librarians might wish to add and corresponding reactive behaviors that could be eliminated.

Proactive behavior added: Serving on committees and teams to know in advance when new demands will be placed on the

TIME MANAGEMENT EXERCISE 18

Adding Proactive Behaviors—20 minutes

1. Review the information on proactive behaviors from Chapters One and Five.
2. Take five minutes. Sit and quietly think. What is one thing that you do that you consider proactive behavior?
3. How does it make your feel when you initiate a proactive activity? Be certain you understand your feelings related to proactive behavior. There is risk taking associated with proactive activities. This can be positive to some people and negative to others. It is important to understand how your feelings influence your choice of proactive behaviors.
4. Choose one type of proactive behavior you would like to add to your management or service activities.
5. Consider carefully how doing this might make you feel. Review the sections on self esteem and assertiveness if necessary before implementing the activity.
6. Choose one corresponding reactive behavior to eliminate.
7. Consider carefully how others might respond to your new behavior. Communicate your intentions clearly with those affected. Practice assertive statements if necessary.
8. Reward yourself for trying no matter what the outcome. Borrow or purchase a book or tape on self esteem, assertiveness or time management.

library collection. This is an information-gathering function to keep you aware and informed of curriculum changes or community needs. It also includes input into these committees about the ways the library can support the committees' work.

Reactive behavior eliminated: Responding to requests for materials or services from committees or teams that do not fit within the library's long-range plans or priorities. Responding to decisions made by others that affect library service and resources but have not involved the library or library staff in the decision making process.

Proactive behavior added: Encouraging positive feelings in yourself, library users, students, coworkers, or volunteers. Developing self-esteem through conscious focus on your self-worth and the worth of others. Practicing positive self-talk and praising others.

Reactive behavior eliminated: Guilt about not doing activities you do not have the time to do and associated stress-related difficulties.

Proactive behavior added: Explaining decisions and priorities to the affected people. Requesting input into establishing priorities. Disseminating information and communicating the goals, priorities, and objectives of the library. Involving staff members, library users, parents, community members, or students in both the creation and communication of priorities and goals. Having others explain library priorities.

Reactive behavior eliminated: Changing prepared activities based on demands by library users. Accepting the validity of others demands over established library program goals.

Proactive behavior added: Conscious choices about how your time is divided, which tasks deserve priority, and the direction of the library for the short and long-term. Using assertive behavior to reinforce your choices.

Reactive behavior eliminated: Interrupting long-term priorities to respond to needs that could be met by others or by you at a more appropriate time.

Focusing on tasks and techniques that are intrinsically motivating to you will increase your chances of success. You will continue working on the activities or ideas that are interesting. Choose a philosophy, technique, or style that has personal appeal. It is important to enjoy what you do, even if attempts at time management involve risk taking. If you are a cautious person, you may need to minimize the risks. If you are a risk taker, then go for whatever seems like fun. It is never necessary to continue a technique or scheme if it generates more problems than help.

Implementation includes:

Clocks, watches, and timers
Computer software
Files, boxes, and labels
Diaries, calendars, and forms
Other techniques

IMPLEMENTATION REVISITED

One of the most exciting features of a new time management book is the different techniques it can provide to help you implement time management. This book has examined specific implementation techniques for To Do lists, interruptions, managing paper, managing people, and planning. Other implementation techniques were provided in the sections on librarian's time use and librarian space use. The cases throughout the book demonstrate implementation techniques for specific problems. This concluding section provides a further list of techniques for you to choose from when you need something slightly different to do, when all your old techniques are boring, or when you just want to make a change.

Implementation techniques for using clocks, watches, and timers provide ways that time keeping can enhance time management. A computers and time management section examines techniques and ideas for using computer software effectively. The section on files, boxes, containers, and labels take another look at managing paper. The section on calendars, diaries, and forms explores implementation activities related to priorities, analysis, and scheduling. A catch-all category of interesting ideas concludes the section. Remember, all ideas are not for everyone. Choose those that you think will work well with your natural preferences. Have fun and enjoy the possibilities!

CLOCKS, WATCHES, AND TIMERS

- Set a timer or an alarm wristwatch to ring after working on a task for 15 minutes.
- Limit the amount of time you spend on an onerous task to five minutes.
- Set a clock or timer to ring at the end of an appointment. Indicate that you must leave for another meeting.
- Set a timer on telephone conversations.
- Set a clock, watch, or timer to ring at the same time every day. Complete a specific task at that time.
- Set a watch or timer and plan for 15 minutes a day. You will be surprised at how long this actually is.
- Get rid of all clocks, watches, and timers for one day or one week. How did you feel?

- Time how long reference interviews take. Do this subtly.
- Time a certain type of interruption. Is it really as long as you perceive?
- When you need to concentrate on a task, set the timer for 30 minutes. Do not work on any other task during that 30 minutes.
- If coworkers' chatting is bothering you, record the precise length of time they spend talking.
- Time how long it takes you to explain how to do a complicated task. Could you create a set of instructions to make this task shorter?
- Set your watch or clock ahead five minutes.
- Set your watch ahead the exact amount of time it takes you to walk or drive to work. You can then leave at the time you need to arrive and still arrive at the correct time.
- Set a clock or watch to ring at half-hour intervals. Get up, walk around, and take deep breaths.
- Set a clock or watch to ring at three random times during the day. Ask yourself, "Is this task what I really need to be doing?"

COMPUTERS AND TIME MANAGEMENT

- Use a computer word processing program for entering your To Do list and creating priorities.
- Buy a computer program such as MacProject for developing long-range projects and objectives.
- Use a data base program for creating and sorting personal filing categories.
- Create an activities checklist in a data base, word processing, or spreadsheet program.
- Complete a daily diary using a word processor.
- Set aside 15 minutes a day to learn a new computer program. Choose a program that provides the maximum effectiveness with the least amount of learning time. Word processing and project organization software are two excellent time investments for librarians.
- If you are a poor or average typist, purchase a keyboarding study program to increase your speed and accuracy. You could also ask a volunteer, assistant, or student to learn the program.
- Consider software programs that can reduce time spent

on certain tasks (e.g., simple graphics programs for creating invitations, posters, and charts). Remember, it will initially take time to learn to use the program.

- Ask a volunteer, library user, student, or another librarian to show you how a software program you are interested in works.
- Purchase a users' guide or video for a difficult piece of software. Often owners' manuals are neither easy to follow nor informative. Second-party users guides can save time.
- Be certain to schedule time to learn to use a new piece of software before you are faced with a deadline for completing a project with it.
- Carefully check the system requirements before purchasing a new piece of software. Be certain your computer system can support what you want to buy.
- Purchase a scheduling program that starts up when you start the computer and indicates what you are to do today.
- Subscribe to a library network or bulletin board service where you can use your computer to compare ideas and problems with other librarians. Call your state library or local district for information on what is available.
- Teach an assistant, volunteer, student, or library professional to develop the library schedule on an appropriate computer program.
- Do your library budget on a spreadsheet. Anticipated budget cuts or changes can be reflected across all categories. "What if" scenarios can be created based on different possible budget changes.
- Create form letters or forms for recurring communications problems such as letters home to parents about overdue materials or scheduling the library for community groups.
- Make backups of all files you create. More time is spent retrieving or recreating lost information than any other single computer activity.

FILES, BOXES, CONTAINERS, AND LABELS

- Purchase brightly colored supplies to help with motivation.
- Label boxes, files, and containers appropriately and immediately, even it means hand labeling.

- Visit a large office supply store and examine all the new possibilities.
- Purchase removable labels so you can make changes easily.
- Try out a new office product at least twice a year.
- Look at library suppliers catalogs, such as Gaylord and Highsmith, for new ideas and products.
- Develop a system for evaluating the personal materials in your file cabinets on a regular basis.
- Use bankers' boxes for storing short-term materials and clearly provide a "dispose by" date.
- Develop a recycling process for used items. Consider becoming a city recycling center.
- Purchase a bright red accordion folder for urgent items. Clean the urgent folder out each day.
- Use a folder in a color you do not like for low-priority items.
- Set aside a box for interesting items you do not know what to do with. When full, recycle the materials, box and all.

CALENDARS, DIARIES, AND FORMS

- Put your To Do lists on colorful and interesting paper.
- Purchase a new type of calendar and use it in a different way.
- Get a personal journal or diary that has an appealing cover.
- Try using a telephone log form.
- Try using a personal communication form.
- Try using a planning form.
- Ask someone else why they use a particular brand of notebook or diary.
- Keep a list of every time you lose something. What do you lose most often? Develop a specific place for putting those items and train yourself through repetition to always return those items to that place.
- Buy a smaller diary or calendar than usual. This will help limit the number of tasks you can put into the space.
- Create your own form for solving a reoccuring problem.
- Purchase an electronic diary, address keeper, or phone dialer.
- Use a diary to keep track of your personal frustrations,

who they are associated with, and how much time they take.
- When you hear a particularly good assertive "no" statement or a statement setting limits, write it in your diary. Adapt and use these in your own communications when relevant.
- Once a month, try out a new form. Evaluate its effectiveness and decide to continue or discontinue use.

MORE IMPLEMENTATION TECHNIQES

- Keep track of the times of day when you feel good and the times of day when you feel low. Schedule difficult tasks and decision making during the good times. Complete routine, clerical, and easier tasks during the low times.
- Visit someone who manages time well. Take notes on what that person does.
- Visit someone who manages time poorly. (Do not tell that person this!) Take notes on what they do.
- Develop a group of peers who can support each other through technology changes.
- Stop worrying about mistakes. Everyone makes mistakes. Learn what you can. Put it behind you and move on.
- Write one personal and one work-related priority in your diary each day. Complete them. In one year you will have completed over 250 personal tasks and 250 work-related tasks (if you take Saturday and Sunday off). This can be a way to focus on balance.
- Reflect on the balance between your personal, home, and work life on the first Monday of each month. Do you feel satisfied with the way things are? If not, think of three reasonable changes you could make.

Changes can be both temporary and permanent:

Temporary change explores
Permanent change commits

MAKING CHANGES

An aspect time management systems discussed in Chapter 2 was making changes. Committing to time management is a commitment to change. Traditional time management approaches sometimes imply that change results instantly in success. This book asks you to consider commitment to change as a more complex activity. There will be long-term commitments resulting in permanent changes based on personal needs and priorities. Permanent changes will be reflected in the way you behave and in the way people respond to you. You may also choose short-term changes and temporary explorations. In an information age, with the world rapidly changing around us, change has become a permanent component in our lifes. Integrating both short-term and long-term change, as a continuing process into a time management system can mean that the system works more effectively.

When you make long-term commitments resulting in permanent changes, there may be ambivalence in your responses. Change can be threatening. Approaching a problem or time management issue from an exploratory perspective can minimize the impact of change. If you think of the activity as temporary, your discomfort from the change may not be as great. For permanent behavior changes, you will need to make permanent adjustments. Decisions about whether the adjustment period is worth the potential benefits must be based on your own needs. The next section explores the differences between temporary and permanent changes. It discusses the need for both and provides examples of the differences.

TEMPORARY CHANGES

You began time management with a commitment to change. This section looks at how to extend that commitment to change in a more playful and experimental way. It begins with examples of things you can change in considering time management, follows through with a way to reflect on the results of the changes, and concludes with a discussion of the effects of change. Temporary changes in relationship to time management can include any of the activities, strategies, techniques, or procedures already discussed in this book. It can also include any other approach you wish to examine—from water aerobics to Zen meditation. Presented below are examples of specific activities you could change to enliven your time management system:

- Change your time management focus from long term to medium range to short term.
- Change the way you handle a specific task (e.g. mail, telephone, questions).

- Stop doing some activity you feel you must do and see what happens.
- Start doing something new that you have always wanted to do.
- Rearrange your schedule—do things in the morning you normally do in the afternoon and completely invert your day.
- Stop making a To Do list if you already use one. Start a To Do list if you do not use one now.
- Do every third item on your To Do list.
- Only attempt activities that seem irrelevant.
- Only attempt activities that seem really difficult.
- Set aside one hour a day to think. Do this for a minimum of one week.
- Keep a journal for two weeks.
- Choose a time management technique you think is silly and try it out.
- Take a traditional time management technique and change it .
- Find a strategy or technique contrary to your basic style. Try it out to see what insights it gives you about personal responses to time.
- Decide to think about time in a different way. For example, rather than thinking about how long it takes to do something, think about how satisfied the results will make you feel.
- Do not do anything related to time management. Continue to read and study until something bubbles to the surface that is so overwhelming you cannot help but try it.
- Have someone suggest a strategy or technique that he or she thinks would be right for you.
- Develop your own change activities and try them out.

Have fun! Try a new way of doing or being on a temporary basis

These changes are meant to be short-term activities that raise your consciousness or awareness. They help examine habitual and repetitive behavior. They give new perspectives on work and actions. Once you have made the change, continue it for a period from two days to two weeks at most. This is meant to be an enjoyable and entertaining activity, to shake up complacency and routine. Be sincere in your attempts, but do not take any results too seriously. When you are done, reflect on the differences the change made.

What difference did the change make?

- How did you feel about making this change?
- What significant consequences did it have for you?
- What significant consequences did it have for others?
- Did anyone comment on the change either negatively or positively? What were their comments?
- What might be the long-term effects of continuing with this change? Do these sound like positive or negative effects?
- What have you learned about the way you manage time from this activity?

Making these changes provides a different focus on what you do and how you do it. It does not have to be permanent. It is a way of exploring the problems you may be having with time management. The more outrageous, unconventional, or uncomfortable the change you make, the more likely you are to have interesting responses. It is a creative, dynamic activity. It is an experiment in time. Have fun, enjoy the change. You can always return to traditional ways if the change turns out to be annoying, difficult, or hard to handle. Making changes for a short time will not make dramatic differences in your time management, but it can provide interesting information. You may discover abilities and feelings about yourself or the people around you that will lead to more permanent changes.

PERMANENT CHANGES

As you make changes in the way you think about time, organize time, and make decisions about time, you will also make changes in the way you behave. The changes discussed above are short term and may result in a few raised eyebrows. They are not significant responses, nor will they result in any significant differences in how people treat you. The permanent changes suggested throughout this book and resulting from a strong commitment to time management will affect other people significantly. It will influence the way coworkers, friends, and family relate to you, the way you relate to others, and even the way you relate to yourself. To integrate time management successfully, you must carefully consider the effect of your new behaviors on others.

As your behavior changes in relationship to time, people

may be surprised. What you are doing will not be familiar to them; it may make them uncomfortable. People have developed expectations about how you usually behave. They may want you to go back to the old ways because they are more comfortable with predictable behavior. It is important to make people aware when you make changes, particularly changes that affect your relationships.

Case of the Puzzled Planner

C.J. decided to set aside 15 minutes at the beginning of each work day to plan. These 15 minutes had usually been set aside for coffee and chatting with other faculty and the library staff. Lynn, one of the library staff members, began to think C.J. did not want to be associated with the staff. This perception made Lynn uncomfortable and, eventually, resentful. When C.J. explained a new check-out procedure Lynn was unattentive and so the explanation took much longer than expected. C.J. was puzzled, as Lynn was usually very quick to learn new procedures.

Chris, a member of the social studies faculty, also noticed that C.J. was not having coffee at the regular time. The teacher decided that C.J. must have a personal problem which could not be talked about in public. After a couple of days, Chris walked directly into C.J.'s office, interrupting a critical planning task, to express concern over the missing coffee break and asked, "What is wrong? Is there anything I can do to help?" C.J. again was puzzled and said, "No, I am working on the new information skills curriculum." The teacher left confused, still wondering what had happened.

C.J.'s original need to establish a few quiet moments to plan resulted in greater time problems. The behavior change affected other people adversely. When C.J. finally asked Lynn what was wrong, the problem was quickly resolved, and they chatted at other times during the day. When the new information skills curriculum was presented at the social studies department meeting, Chris realized what C.J. had been doing. Later they shared the misunderstanding and laughed about it.

C.J. discovered through these confusions how important it was to keep people informed. The next time C.J. made a change, all people to be affected were told. Improved communications helped others understand and respect C.J.'s decisions. The benefits were worth the time spent explaining a behavior change to staff, colleagues, and friends.

Permanent changes in time management may result in

TIME MANAGEMENT EXERCISE 19

Making Changes—45 minutes

1. Identify one temporary and one permanent change you have made in the past six months.
2. What was the reason for the temporary change? Was it meant to be temporary or did you just not follow through? Try to remember how you felt.
3. What was the reason for the permanent change? How did you sustain motivation to make it permanent? How do you feel about this change?
4. Write, tape record or videotape a brief statement about how you feel about change. Is it challenging? Distressing? Difficult? Fun? Exciting?
5. Read, listen or view your statement again in four months.

different social as well as personal priorities. The time you spend with family and friends may increase because your use of time will match more closely with your personal priorities. Often family and personal life are at the top of your priority list, but the least amount of time is committed to them. Serious commitment to change will result in the time you spend reflecting your personal values more closely. For example, you may spend less time in work-related social situations which you considered essential in the past. If time with family and friends is important, you will make that a reality and bring time commitment more in line with activities that result in personal satisfaction. This will improve the balance between your personal values and the way you implement them in your life and work.

Changing the way you look at and respond to time is a permanent commitment. Increasing self-esteem can be reflected in your choices of how you use time. As you believe more strongly in yourself, you will believe more in your ability to make well-founded decisions about time. You will change the way you think about yourself. Increased self-esteem means increased self-confidence and self-respect. This will result in permanent changes not only in the way you deal with time but also in the way you deal with yourself and those around you.

IMPORTANCE OF TIME MANAGEMENT

One of the most often-asked questions about time management is, "Why is it important? Couldn't everything I need to know about time management be written up in one or two pages? After all, isn't it just making lists and keeping track of what I do? What's the matter with me? If I just concentrate, it shouldn't be that difficult!" Time management is a phrase that represents many relationships and problems. When shortened to a two-word phrase it seems manageable. When closely examined, as has been done in this book, the complexities and difficulties become more apparent. Time management is neither simple nor a solution to all problems. By approaching time management from the perspectives of creating balance, achieving satisfaction in personal and professional priorities, and developing self-esteem, it can be seen as important and relevant.

Time management, in today's society, is not "fixing" people to make them more efficient. This is not the industrial age governed by a mechanical perspective. Time management must be personal and must result in personal development. The purpose of time management is not to try and do more in each day by increasing production. The importance of time management is to integrate and balance the priorities of our personal and professional lives—to be happier, healthier and more satisfied.

What are the real reasons time management is worth bothering about?

Can time management do these things for you?

- Increase personal happiness and satisfaction.
- Promote activities and ideas you believe make a difference.
- Present consistent responses to library users, faculty, staff, community members, students, or coworkers.
- Reduce frustration, anxiety, and stress in yourself and in others.
- Balance feelings of need to do against what may be accomplished.
- Help others to become happier and more satisfied.
- Enjoy life more.

TIME MANAGEMENT EXERCISE 20

Why is Time Management Important?

1. Take five minutes and write down as many reasons as you can think of that indicate why you want to improve your time management.
2. Review the list and add anything else you think of.
3. Using three different colored pens or markers, circle the work reasons, the personal reasons and the family/friends reasons why improved time management would be useful to you.
4. Is there a balance between the three areas in your list?
5. Sit quietly and think about your reasons and the proportion in each area. Are you satisfied?
6. Make a positive self statement at the end of this exercise.

- Complete important projects and activities.
- Be able to say no and not feel guilty.

There are probably many other reasons you can think of why time management would be personally useful. Exercise 20 provides a method for you to develop your own list of why time management is important.

TIME MANAGEMENT AND BEYOND

Time management provides balance for librarians' personal and professional choices

Time management is not a problem that will ever be completely solved. There will always be too many demands, too many things to do. We can learn to be content and comfortable with the choices we have made. We can know that from among available options we have chosen what we believe will be the best use of our time and the time of those we influence. It is a combination of self-awareness, self-esteem, planning, assertiveness, and self-discovery that works together to help realize time values.

Time management can be a pedestrian method for making superficial changes. Any improvements that result, however, are useful and important if they reflect an underlying need to make stronger and more permanent changes. Do not stop with the trivial and mechanistic. Look beyond to ways to make life better.

Time management can also be a voyage of self-discovery, an attempt to make life more meaningful and work more important. As librarians we are in the position to make both our dreams and other people's dreams possible. We have the power to make life better. We make a substantial difference to the community we serve through our abilities to access information, organize, evaluate, synthesize, and understand.

BIBLIOGRAPHY

Alberti, R. E., and M. L. Emmons. 1990. *Your perfect right: A guide to assertive living*. 6th ed. San Luis Obispo, Calif.: Impact Publishers.

American Association of School Librarians. 1988. *A planning guide for information power: Guidelines for school library media programs*. Chicago: American Association of School Librarians.

Blanchard, K. 1990. *One minute manager* (audio, 2 cassettes). Boulder, Colo.: CareerTrack Publications.

Blanchard, K. and W. Oncken. 1988. *One minute manager meets the monkey* (audio, 120 minutes). New York: Simon and Schuster Sound Ideas.

———. 1989. *One minute manager meets the monkey*. New York: William Morrow.

Bliss, E. C. 1986. *Doing it now* (audio, 50 minutes). New York: Simon and Schuster Sound Ideas.

———. 1991. *Getting things done: The ABC's of time management.* New York: Charles Scribner's Sons.

Branden, N. 1987. *How to raise your self-esteem*. New York: Bantam.

———. 1990. *Master true self-esteem* (audio, 60 minutes). New York: Bantam Audio Productions.

Caputo, J. S. 1984. *Assertive librarian*. Phoenix: Oryx Press.

Davidson, J. 1991. *Breathing space: Living and working at a comfortable pace in a sped-up society*. New York: MasterMedia Limited.

Dodd, A. W. 1987. *Practical strategies for taming the paper and people problems in teaching*. Springfield, Ill.: Charles C. Thomas Publisher.

Elgin, S. H. 1990. *Mastering the gentle art of verbal self-defense* (audio, 60 minutes). New York: Simon and Schuster Audio.

Eyre, R. M. and L. Eyre. 1987. *LifeBalance: Priority balance, attitude balance, goal balance in all areas of your life*. New York: Ballantine.

Goldstein, A., ed. 1988. *J. K. Lasser's executive's personal organizer forms*. New York: J. K. Lasser Tax Institute.

Harris, D. 1985. *The Woman's Day guide to organizing your life*. New York: Holt, Rinehart and Winston.

Haynes, M. E. 1987. *Personal time management*. Los Altos, Calif.: Crisp Publications.

Hemphill, B. 1988. *Taming the paper tiger: Organizing the paper in your life*. New York: Dodd, Mead & Company.

Hobbs, C. R. 1987. *Time power*. New York: Harper Row.

Hunt, D., and P. Hait. 1990. *Tao of time*. New York: Henry Holt and Co.

Januz, L. R., and S. K. Jones. 1981. *Time-Management for executives: A handbook from the Editors of ExecuTime*. New York: Charles Scribners Sons.

Johnson, S. 1985. *One minute for myself*. New York: Avon.

Lakein, A. 1973. *How to get control of your time and your life*. New York: Peter H. Wyden, Inc.

LeBoeuf, M. 1979. *Working smart: How to accomplish more in half the time*. New York: Warner Books.

———. 1987. *Working smarter* (audio, 60 minutes). Chicago: Nightingale-Conant Corporation.

Lebov, M. 1980. *Practical tools and techniques for managing time*. Englewood Cliffs, NJ: Prentice-Hall.

Lundberg, C. C. 1984. Zero-In: A technique for formulating better mission statements. *Business Horizons*. 27: 30-33.

McCay, J. T. 1959. *Management of time*. Englewood Cliffs, NJ: Prentice-Hall, Inc.

Mackenzie, A. 1984. *How to set priorities* (audio, 51 minutes). Greenwich, Conn.: Listen USA.

———. 1988. *Time to sell* (audio). Chicago: Dartnell.

———. 1990. *Teamwork through time management*. Chicago: Dartnell.

———, and K. C. Waldo, Kay Cronkite. 1981. *About time! A woman's guide to time management.* New York: McGraw Hill.

Mayer, J. J. 1990. *If you haven't got the time to do it right, when will you find the time to do it over*? New York: Simon and Schuster.

Morrisey G. L., P. J. Below and B. L. Acomb. 1988. *Executive guide to operational planning*. San Francisco: Jossey-Bass.

Oncken, W. 1984. *Managing management time: Who's got the monkey*? Englewood Cliffs, NJ: Prentice-Hall.

Riggs, D. D. 1984. *Strategic planning for library managers*. Phoenix: Oryx Press.

Schlenger, S., and R. Roesch. 1989. *How to be organized in spite of yourself.* New York: New American Library.

Seivert, L. J. 1989. *Time is money: Save it!* Homewood, Ill.: Dow-Jones Irwin.

Shipman, N. J., J. B. Martin, A. B. McKay and R. E. Anastasi. 1983. *Effective time-management techniques for school administrators*. Englewood Cliffs, NJ: Prentice-Hall.

Silcox, D., and M. E. Moore. 1980. *Woman time: Personal time management for women only*. Wyden Books.

Silver, S. 1991. *Organized to be the best*! 2nd ed. Los Angeles: Adams-Hall Publishing.

Skopec, E. W., and L. Kiely. 1991. *Taking charge: Time management for personal and professional productivity*. Reading, Mass.: Addison-Wesley.

Webber, R. A. 1992. *Breaking your time barrier: Being a strategic time manager*. Englewood Cliffs, NJ: Prentice-Hall.

Weiss, D. H. 1986. *Get organized! How to control your life through self management*. New York: Amacom.

Winston, S. 1983. *The organized executive: New ways to manage time, paper and people*. New York: Norton.

———. 1989. *The organized executive: New ways to manage time, paper and people* (audio, 6 cassettes). New York: Simon and Schuster Sound Ideas.

INDEX

Dr. Dian Walster is Coordinator of the Library Media Program for the Division of Instructional Technology, School of Education, University of Colorado, Denver.

Dr. Barbara L. Stein is Associate Professor at the School of Library and Information Science at the University of North Texas. She has experience both as a school teacher and a media specialist.

Cover design: Apicella Design
Typography: C. Roberts